# FAIRY HOUSES

## How to Create Whimsical Homes for Fairy Folk

Sally J. Smith

COOL
SPRINGS
PRESS

MINNEAPOLIS, MINNESOTA

Quarto is the authority on a wide range of topics.

Quarto educates, entertains and enriches the lives of our readers—enthusiasts and lovers of hands-on living.

www.quartoknows.com

First published in 2017 by Cool Springs Press, an imprint of Quarto Publishing Group USA Inc., 400 First Avenue North, Suite 400, Minneapolis, MN 55401 USA. Telephone: (612) 344-8100 Fax: (612) 344-8692

quartoknows.com
Visit our blogs at quartoknows.com

Cool Springs Press titles are also available at discounts in bulk quantity for industrial or sales-promotional use. For details contact the Special Sales Manager at Quarto Publishing Group USA Inc., 400 First Avenue North, Suite 400, Minneapolis, MN 55401 USA.

10 9 8 7 6 5 4 3 2 1

ISBN: 978-1-59186-672-5

Library of Congress Cataloging-in-Publication Data
Names: Smith, Sally J., 1954– author.
Title: Fairy houses : how to create whimsical homes for fairy folk / Sally J. Smith.
Description: Minneapolis, MN, USA : Quarto Publishing Group USA Inc., 2017.
Identifiers: LCCN 2016033755 | ISBN 9781591866725 (plc)
Subjects: LCSH: Nature craft. | Fairies in art. | Dollhouses.
Classification: LCC TT157 .S543 2017 | DDC 745.592/3—dc23
LC record available at https://lccn.loc.gov/2016033755

Acquiring Editor: Mark Johanson
Creative Director: Laura Drew
Project Manager: Alyssa Bluhm
Art Direction and Cover Design: Cindy Samargia Laun
Book Design: Amelia LeBarron
Book Layout: Wendy Holdman

Printed in China

# CONTENTS

4   DEDICATION

5   ACKNOWLEDGMENTS

7   INTRODUCTION

9   CHAPTER 1
INSPIRATIONS: DESIGNING WITH NATURE

37   CHAPTER 2
BLUEPRINT FOR A FAERIE HOUSE

53   CHAPTER 3
ITTY BITTY NITTY GRITTY: CREATING
MAGICAL FAERIE HOUSE COMPONENTS

101   CHAPTER 4
ADDING TWINKLE AND STYLE:
LIGHTING AND INTERIORS

127   CHAPTER 5
FINISHING TOUCHES: ROOFS, BASES,
AND EXTERIOR DETAILS

163   CHAPTER 6
BUILDING A FAERIE HOUSE FROM THE
GROUND, UP

186   INDEX

190   ABOUT THE AUTHOR

192   CONVERSIONS

# DEDICATION

This book is dedicated to the living earth and the visible and invisible beings with whom we share this extraordinary place we all call home.

In memoriam, this book is also dedicated to my dear feline companion Oliver, whose endless patience and love are intermingled in mysterious ways with many of the creations you will find in these pages.

Oliver was no ordinary cat. For the past 14 years he accompanied me on many of my building and gathering forays into the forest and in all sorts of weather. He was especially fond of the crisp, cold days of winter. His playfulness helped keep me lighthearted and his animal instincts helped keep me open to the subtle changes in the forest around us. He brought joy and delight to each and every step out our front door. He was often by my side as I made many of the images in this book, inspecting the faerie houses and adding his comments when he felt they were needed.

So it was a great shock when, just as this book was finished, his life also came to a close. Oliver's journey done, he slipped away peacefully in my arms, in the garden on a beautiful late summer day.

Blessed be one and all.

# ACKNOWLEDGMENTS

There are so many people I wish to thank who have helped make this book:

- **Katie Elzer-Peters**, who was given the impossible job of editor, coach, cheerleader, and head-weeder, and did it all with cheerfulness, professionalism, and enthusiasm. Thank you, Katie!

- **Jonathan Gunson**, who encouraged me from the very first Milkweed House.

- **My father**, whose last words to me were to keep making faerie houses because it was important.

- **My mother**, who gave me life and a love of gardens and flowers.

- **My sisters**, who had to put off so much while I worked on this.

- **Elizabeth**, who taught me to take care of what I was given.

- **Hilary Matthews**—supporter-in-chief and fellow wild-woman.

- **Paul Wheeler at LGL**—for several decades of first-rate friendship and professional representation.

- **Derek Muirden**, who shot hours of faerie house videos in the magical light of the Adirondacks for his PBS show and became a good friend in the process.

- **Leslie and Aleta at Amber Lotus** for making my work look *so* good.

- **The "other": SJS, Stephen**, who gave me the tools I needed to get started and helped keep the magic alive, along with **MM**, his wife, who is the epitome of tenacity.

- **The Sisters of the Sacred Vessel**, who supported me with unconditional love and support for this project—you helped more than you know.

- **To Jon Hancock** for phenomenal technical support and faith in me as an artist.

- **To dear friends Robyn, Robert, Davie, and many others** . . . you know who you are.

- **To all my many fans, Kickstarter supporters, and customers** who helped keep the lights on and the computer(s) humming (even after the first one died).

- **To you, dear reader**, who knows that there is still plenty of magic left in the world and who wants to make some more.

I am most grateful to the Invisible Beings who live with us every day and who guide me to secret places of beauty and magic, who protect me out in the wilderness while I work, and who make their presence known to anyone who will take the time to slow down and pay attention. This book could not exist without their gentle presence.

This book is definitely a different kind of faerie book. It will take you from the world of dreams and imagination right down to the earth by way of practical matters—learning how to actually construct and build detailed faerie house creations of your very own. It's filled with nuts and bolts, practical information, and step-by-step guides that teach you how to build your own enchanting creations.

I've written this book with the skillful crafter in mind. If you've never made anything with your hands before, you may find the tutorials in these pages a bit challenging, so start with the beginner projects. If you have some experience with putting things together, this book will open new doors of creativity for you.

Our main focus will be houses built in the craft studio (not outdoors), though I will cover some of the basics of outdoor constructions. This book presents basic faerie house construction as a series of steps or phases. First, you'll make the small elements, such as windows and doors. Then you'll construct the main body of the house. Finally, you'll put it all together and place it in the landscape. It may *sound* simple, but there are *loads* of tricks and detailed techniques that I share in this book to make the projects easier for you. I've developed these over the past decade with practice, trial, and error, so you don't have to make the same mistakes.

A word to parents of crafty kids: This book may be suitable for talented older kids, as well as young adults who want to learn more about this subject. I find that young people learn a great deal about structure, form, design, and ingenuity by taking up the craft of faerie house building. Perhaps they are budding architects or engineers in the making, or stage designers or movie-makers trying to develop their dreams and visions. If so, this book may be helpful to them because we cover various construction methods in miniature that they may be able to apply to their own creative projects. These houses are works of art, however—not toys—and should be treated as such.

I've written this book as I would speak if we were sitting together in my studio and I was guiding you through your very own project. I hope that learning some of these simple skills and methods will enable and embolden you to take your creativity as far as you want. It is satisfying to make these little structures, and everyone always benefits from more magic and creativity in their lives!

# inspirations

DESIGNING WITH NATURE

Whether you bring your tools and build onsite or take a few photos and go home to conjure and create the perfect dwelling for the space you've discovered, it's always best to take your creative cues from the natural world around you. As you look to nature for inspiration and building supplies, you may also find that unexpected things happen, like discovering a perfect faerie nook. Perhaps this is the faerie folk letting you know they approve!

Inspired by the tiger lilies that grace my garden every year, I built this tiny house to be enjoyed by the faeries when the flowers are in full bloom.

OPPOSITE:
**The Cedar
Basket House.**
This ephemeral
structure encloses
the charming space
nestled between the
trunks of a few white
cedars. It is made
entirely from materials
found nearby. The
mushrooms were not
present when the
house was built, but
when I returned the
next day to take the
photos, they had all
magically appeared.
Sometimes delightful
things happen when
we play respectfully
with nature.

LEFT:
**Autumn Leaf Gazebo.**
This observation
gazebo perched over
the small waterfall
provides for ideal
viewing of red and
golden autumn leaves
drifting downstream.
The bridge made
from pinned-together
autumn leaves ensures
that only the light-
footed will be able
to visit.

INSPIRATIONS

RIGHT:
**The Golden Door.**
Sometimes a tiny space can be transformed with a simple addition. I made this doorway in the studio using eco-friendly glues and techniques so that it could be left in the tree roots for others to enjoy.

OPPOSITE:
**Emerald Moss House.**
Some locations just beckon to us with possibilities. This site along a remote trail was such a location. The stone house took a week to make with all locally sourced materials, but all the moss was already there. Sharp-eyed hikers enjoyed finding the house for several years until nature claimed it back.

## STUDIO-BUILT HOUSES INSTALLED OUTDOORS

When you're learning to build faerie houses, crafting in the studio is easiest. If you have a particular destination in mind for your faerie dwelling, take some measurements before you build. That way you'll know the house will fit in your chosen location.

ABOVE: **Fernwood Cottage.** I created this rustic cottage in the studio for this particular location—tucked under a clump of maidenhair ferns (my favorite). There were moments when dappled sunlight filtering through the leaf canopy high above the woodland garden caught the edges of the cottage and brought the whole scene to life.

OPPOSITE: **The Bellflower House.** A rugged alpine cliff festooned with wildflowers was the perfect location for this unusual house made from birch bark. After taking the photos, I brought the house home with me to be used in a different setting years later.

OPPOSITE: **The Adirondack Faerie Lodge.**
This house weighed 20 pounds due to the stone foundation and was a challenge to haul up the mountain! I replanted the cushion mosses back in my garden (where I got them) after the photo shoot.

ABOVE: **High-Summer Cottage Garden House.**
A neighbor's garden bursting with color inspired this rather formal home with blue-glazed windows that match the blue blossoms in the background. Imagine looking out the windows of this house and seeing the daisies so close!

ABOVE: **The Dogwood Chateau.** Tucked under some fragrant balsam branches, this tiny house glows with welcoming wonder. Some houses can manage a few days in cold and snow (if the snow is dry), but for the most part, scenes like this are created for the moment and live on only in photos. This house now lives next to a stone fireplace in a lovely home, where it looks equally magical.

OPPOSITE: **The Beach House.** Using materials collected from beaches from around the world and recycling a previously used house (can you find it in these pages?), I created a sumptuous beach house dwelling for a few days of high summer enjoyment.

## ASSEMBLED ONSITE WITH STUDIO-BUILT COMPONENTS

It's a deep pleasure to work onsite and go with the flow of natural nooks and crannies, interesting building materials, or particularly magical spaces you happen upon. To make creations that are even more satisfying, try bringing a few premade components, such as doors and windows, with you to enhance your projects. The pre-made elements add a lot of detail and save on construction time, which can be limited when working outside.

**Brookwater Pavilion.** This Japanese-style teahouse made with ferns and flowers is even more charming with the addition of the birch-bark walkway.

**The Hosta Treehouse.** This house was custom built for this location. The two shelf mushrooms were alive and attached to this tree, as were the ivy strands growing up the trunk. The main house, lower door, and balcony were separate elements designed to rest upon the fungus. Live flowers and leaves give it a bright finish.

**Marsh House.** I made much of this structure in pieces ahead of time, but I found the roof finial and the door's bark decoration near the site. I sourced all of the twig supports and platform from the edges of the pond and built onsite. This was a difficult location for building because the beaver pond was so deep!

**Mossy Manor House.** I made all of the windows and the tower for the house after finding this moss-covered stump. I collected the shelf mushroom awnings, as well as the red berries and flowers, nearby, and made the door onsite. This house is a lovely celebration of the forest's bounty.

**Stonewood Cottage.** The front wall of the house and the tower were built ahead of time for this lush location. I collected flowers, berries, and accent stones nearby and built all of the leaf roofs onsite, pinning them together with thorns.

# WILDCRAFTING: FAERIE HOUSE BUILDING ONSITE

This is the most elemental state of faerie house building, and one that you'll enjoy more as you gain experience. It is possible to build charming dwellings with nothing but the materials you find scattered about. While you're likely to mostly make faerie houses indoors, it's fun to occasionally craft a surprise dwelling outdoors for an unsuspecting faerie (or person) to stumble upon.

**Stone Garden Hut.** This house is made with dry-laid stones, just like human-scaled stonework. These houses, however, are a bit of an illusion because they're not really hollow on the inside. Stone houses last longer and are easier to build if they are constructed as solid structures that give the illusion of having an interior. You can do this by placing a dark stone behind the door window and creating a deep window well for the round window. This house lasted through several harsh winters because it was solid and well built.

I love working with flowers—they just naturally seem like places faeries would have tea or take a nap. The following are a few of my favorite flower houses.

**The Tulip Tea House.** Made from a single spring tulip, daffodils, and red fern fronds, this delicate house perched in a miniature rhododendron seems like a perfect place to sip some Faerie Tea.

Part of the adventure of building in the wild is searching for special locations. You never know what you may find out in the woods, in a park, or in your own backyard. Seeing new potential in simple materials or settings is part of the learning curve. The more you let yourself explore and create, the more you will see each time you venture out looking for magical experiences and materials.

OPPOSITE: **Spring Gazebo.** Hidden in the spring border garden is this delicate gazebo made with pussy willow twigs and spring blossoms all bursting forth from a tuffet of cushion moss.

ABOVE: **Dogwood Duplex.** On a moss-lined bank of a quiet river, this little stone structure seemed to just build itself. I collected all materials within a 100' stretch of the river: driftwood, stones, shells, and birch bark. I came back the next day and saw that someone else had added some extra decorations, which delighted me completely.

OPPOSITE: **Forest Moss Palace.** A lush, moss-covered stump was the base for this 30"-tall creation. The ground cedars (a protected species) were already there, which made the spot irresistible for embellishing.

ABOVE: **Rivertwig House.** Delicate autumn twigs, grasses, and milkweed pods are arranged in an unusual house that moves gracefully in the wind. Milkweed pods make excellent faerie boats too!

ABOVE: **Riverstone Tower.** This 3'-tall stone tower was made entirely from materials collected along the river. It took three to four days to build but was enjoyed by many, as a nearby bridge allowed everyone to easily see the project.

OPPOSITE: **The Ice Queen's Palace.** I collected icicles from the shores of a freezing lake to make this house. Ice sticks together very well with a little bit of water and snow when the temperatures are between 22° and 28°F. Just hold the ice in place while it sets. Go slowly and carefully while building and you can create glittering palaces with surprising ease.

Faerie house building out in nature does not have to stop in winter. Some of my favorite houses are made from ice and snow.

Ready to build? The next chapter outlines the tools and materials you will need to make fabulous faerie creations.

# CHAPTER 2

# Blueprint for a faerie House

An extravagant Faerie Château perched on the edge of a quiet lake is kissed by morning light. Sustainably harvested cypress knees make excellent bases for treehouse-type constructions.

Before we can get down to the basics of building, I need to teach you about the various elements, processes, and materials used in faerie house construction. The ultimate location where you plan to place your faerie house will impact the design and materials used, as will your skill level. Here are some essential tips to help you orient yourself as you design your first creation.

## LOCATION! LOCATION! LOCATION!

The first place to start in discussing the building of faerie houses is to consider whether you want to work strictly outdoors or if you want to create your house in a studio or indoor location.

### OUTDOOR FAERIE HOUSES

Building faerie houses outdoors with materials found right in the immediate area results in sculptures that are spontaneous and fun but not very durable. "Locally sourced" takes on a whole new meaning when you are looking at stumps, forest floors, or other natural locations for building materials. A general rule of thumb is to collect respectfully and leave living materials in place untouched. While it is

Items built to be left outdoors *must* be constructed using only natural materials and non-toxic glues, which means using no hot glue or glue guns. This glue is made from plastic, so it will not degrade and can cause harm to wildlife. *Please* work respectfully if you are going to leave your studio-made embellishment outside permanently.

true that some of my images contain fresh-collected leaves and flowers, I always did so following sustainable practices and asked permission first . . . even from the plants themselves. Sometimes, even if they are plentiful, a tree may not wish to share its leaves. Consult your intuition and respect the answer that comes.

These little creations are naturally ephemeral as they come from the earth and return to it. It's likely you'll make your little house and enjoy it for a bit, only to leave it for others to discover while it still stands.

Oftentimes the site itself will help guide that process.

When building outdoors, you can bring premade elements, such as doors or windows, with you. I like doing this because it adds creativity and sophistication to the design. Some things are difficult to make

Once you start creating, you'll find inspiration everywhere—such as this moss- and fungi-covered tree.

Here is the same location with the addition of a few twigs and leaves. Sometimes less is more.

out in the field but can be made in the studio ahead of time. I keep a stash of premade items in a basket to take into the woods with me. It is great fun to work this way!

Making houses for different seasons gives us fabulous opportunities to expand our creative expression.

This studio-built door turned into a perfect faerie portal.

When this real pumpkin house began to collapse, I retrieved the door and window to be used again in a different house. Can you find them in these pages? If you want to create a permanent pumpkin house, make or buy a faux pumpkin to use as your base.

A festive holiday house made from a hollowed-out pomegranate. I used hawthorn thorns to pin the doorframe and awning in place. I used eco-glue to make the window lattice ahead of time and used more thorns to pin the latticework to the inside of the windows. Holly covers the top opening. Because the house was 100 percent natural, I left it for the woodland faeries to enjoy.

## INDOOR FAERIE HOUSES

Building a faerie house indoors in a controlled environment with lots of tools, pre-gathered or purchased materials, and plenty of time allows you to make one-of-a-kind, truly amazing artistic creations. Houses that will be kept safely indoors (with an occasional visit to the garden) can be made with more durable components and adhesives, and with more luxurious decorative elements such as battery-powered lights, sparkly glass beads, velvet leaves, wallpapers, and so forth.

## SELECTING A HOUSE STYLE

After choosing a location (indoors or outdoors), decide whether the house will have round/curved walls or flat ones. There are construction challenges to each design style. For example, doors and windows are a bit more difficult to install on curved walls. Flat-walled houses require more creativity on your part to ensure that they don't look like miniature human houses. Once you've had a little experience with each, you will feel comfortable using either design format.

Here are some examples to illustrate the point.

TOP ROW: A round-walled house with and without its roof.

BOTTOM ROW: A flat-walled house with and without its roof.

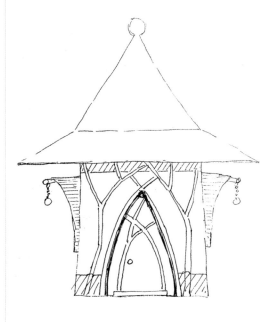

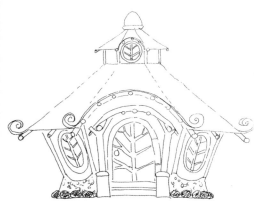

Here are two sketches for the houses you'll learn how to build in Chapter 6.

## DESIGNING & BUILDING A FAERIE DREAM HOME

Once you have decided whether to use curved or flat wall construction, it's helpful to make a quick sketch of the house so you know where you plan to put doors, windows, and towers on your house. You should also think about the type of roof you'd like to build.

Once the sketch is done, you can gather your materials. Select interesting materials to inspire construction—perhaps a particular twisted branch, a lovely jewelry finding, or a special shell or stone that you've found. Don't worry about having absolutely everything on hand before you begin, as part of the process—the adventure of creating—is going out to find additional bits for your project to enhance its design.

When you have a basic plan for your faerie house, you'll follow these general steps to build it.

1. Select and prepare the wall materials, as well as the base—if the house will have one.
2. Create the individual elements for the house such as doors, windows, vestibules, towers, porches, and so forth. It is much easier to create these elements separately ahead of time and add them to the body of the house.
3. Install the doors and windows while keeping in mind whether the house is to be finished on the inside or not, if lighting will be added or not, and if the roof will be removable or not.
4. Attach towers, bay or bump-out windows, decorative outside features (such as vines and twig trim), and prepare for the roof attachment.
5. Install lighting, keeping the battery pack handy (but as hidden as possible) so it's easy to operate the switch and change the batteries, when needed.
6. Finish the interior walls, including decorative elements and trims, lighting sconces, window seat upholstery, and so forth. Final finishing is done at this step if the house will have a fixed roof. If the roof will be removable, finishing can be done later.
7. Build the roof(s). Build attached roofs directly onto the house. Build removable roofs separately. Add dormers, towers, chimneys, and finials that are part of the roof. Finish the inside of the roof if it will be removable.

8. Create and install the floor for the house. If a fixed roof has been installed, this will be your final chance to make any adjustments to the interior of the house before it is sealed up. For removable-roof houses, adding the floor is usually completed before the final interior finishes are done.

9. Add final landscaping details to the house. If you desire to attach the house to a base, do that now as well, and landscape around the base.

Chapter 6 will show you step-by-step instructions for house building.

The base of the house adds just as much to the overall look and feel as the rest of the elements. Learn more about constructing bases in Chapter 5.

## FAERIE HOUSE TOOLKITS

If you're like me, you're always going to want to have your faerie house toolkit handy because you never know when inspiration might strike! There are certain tools, such as hand pruners, that I always carry when I'm walking about, looking for materials or building faerie houses in nature. Other items, including things like glue guns and epoxy resin, are only used indoors, so I have two different toolkits with a few items that are common to both. Because building out in nature requires respect for the environment, I tend to use a lot of thorns, raffia, and cotton/linen thread to hold things together, as they will eventually break down and return to nature.

Let's take a peek at my outdoor kit first.

## OUTDOOR TOOLKIT

There are a few more tools in my kit that I bring with me that are not in this image because they are larger, but I always bring them with me and I'm happy that I have them when I work in the woods. They are:

- Leather gloves
- Small foam kneeling pad
- Collecting bags or baskets
- Notebook and pen

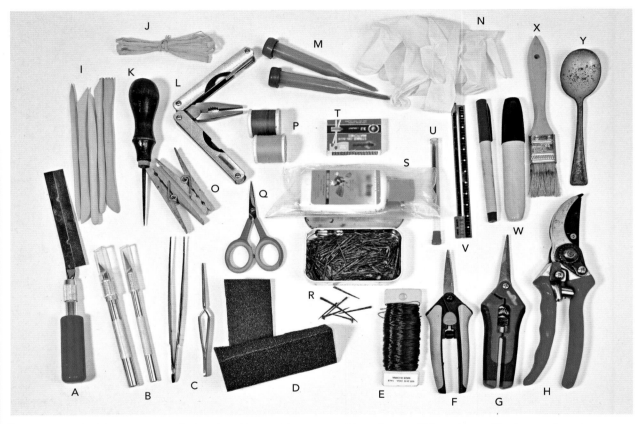

(A) Fine-toothed flat saw, (B) small, sharp hand knives, (C) tweezers, (D) sandpaper, (E) florist's wire, (F) micro garden snips, (G) long-nosed garden snips, (H) hand pruners, (I) wooden clay sculpting tools, (J) raffia or other natural fiber twines and heavy threads, (K) awl, (L) folding multi-tool device, (M) florist's water piks, (N) surgical gloves—mandatory for mushroom handling, (O) wooden clothespins—helpful for holding things together during assembly, (P) cotton thread—various seasonal colors to blend in with seasonal foliage, (Q) small scissors, (R) hawthorne thorns—my essential fastening method for outdoor creating, (S) natural insect repellent, (T) safety matches—only for emergencies, (U) assorted sewing needles—for stitching and sewing items together in the field, (V) small ruler—to help estimate distances during construction, (W) marker pens, (X) 1"-wide natural bristle brush—for sweeping and cleaning the site, (Y) large, old spoon—for digging and landscaping the site.

## STUDIO TOOLKIT

The toolkit for studio work contains more carving, cutting, and sculpting tools as well as various kinds of adhesives. Below is my basic set of tools that I use in the studio.

Tools not shown but part of my studio collection:

- Flat, fine-toothed draw saw
- Coping saw—essential for cutting plywood bases
- Small hand drill and bits

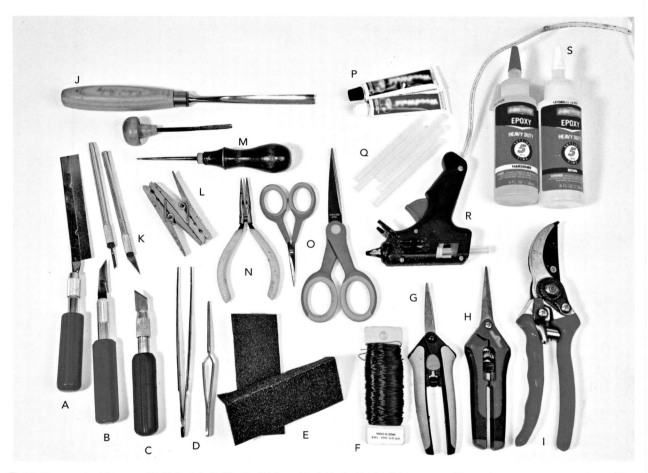

(A) Fine-toothed flat saw, (B) 2" flat-bladed knife, (C) flat, chisel-bladed knife, (D) tweezers, (E) sandpaper in many sizes/grits, (F) florist's wire, (G) micro garden snips, (H) long-nosed garden snips, (I) hand pruners, (J) wood carving gouges—fine and extra-fine sizes, (K) fine and extra-fine craft knives, (L) wooden clothespins, (M) awl, (N) needle-nosed pliers, (O) regular and fine-point scissors, (P) wood-colored two-part epoxy adhesive, (Q) 4" glue sticks for hot glue gun, (R) hot glue gun, (S) clear epoxy resin, 2-part resin.

When sourcing materials, always keep the idea of scale in mind. What might be a tiny bead on the end of an earring could serve as a full-sized doorknob for a faerie house. Choose materials that look harmonious together in terms of size, and that will help you recreate a tiny world. Mostly, think small.

# BUILDING MATERIALS

Let your imagination run wild! Between your backyard and your neighborhood craft store, you should be able to find everything you need to create all manner of magical faerie dwellings.

## COLLECTING MATERIALS FROM THE WILD

Take a look at the inspiration pictures to see what you can collect to build your faerie house. Dried mushrooms, twigs, bark, lichens, seed pods, and leaves can all help enhance your project and make it more inviting for faerie folk.

Keep these tips in mind while collecting materials:

- Never pull bark off of a living tree, as it can cause irreparable and irreversible damage to the tree.
- Collect first on your own property, and always ask for permission when collecting on someone else's. Follow all city, state, and federal laws for removing items from public property.
- If removing material from living plants, such as leaves from a tree, never take more than 5 percent of the overall plant mass. (That is likely to be much more than you would ever possibly need.) Ask permission from the plant first before collecting. *Never* collect protected or endangered plants.

Here are some of my favorite building materials.

**Twigs and branches.**

These are twigs and branches that I commonly use. Of course, what is available in your area may be different. Whenever possible, collect twigs and branches that have already been shed naturally. Make friends with your local garden center so that you can stop by when they're pruning. This can be an excellent source for beautiful and unusual twigs, vines, and branches.

Fresh twigs and small branch cuttings can be bent and shaped into positions that will be useful for construction purposes later once they have dried. For example, bend dogwood or willow stems into complete circles and wire them together. The twigs will then dry in that shape and be useful for windows later on. You can also make arches for doorways this way. It takes a bit of planning, but the natural-looking results are worth it.

Here are some of the many different kinds of twigs and branches that go into making my faerie houses.

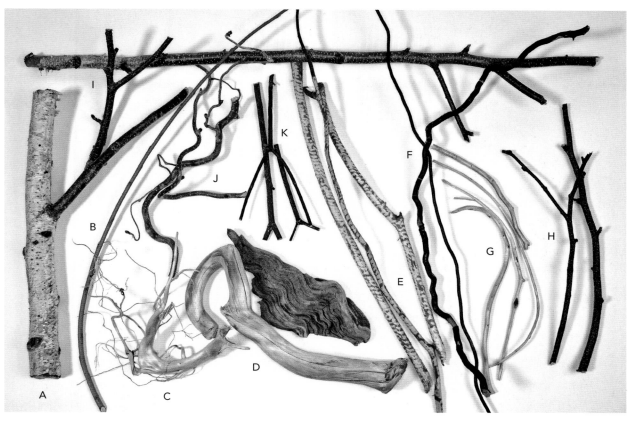

(A) White birch branch with dark twigs, (B) flame willow branch, (C) white cedar root, (D) driftwood, (E) willow twigs, (F) roots, (G) white cedar twigs, (H) birch twigs, (I) birch branches , (J) corkscrew hazel twigs, (K) redosier dogwood twigs.

## KEEPING IT TOGETHER: A FEW WORDS ABOUT GLUE

There are three main types of glue that you'll use to build your faerie house creations.

**For studio-building use:**

**Hot glue:** Primarily used for temporarily anchoring pieces in place while you build. Usually reinforced by epoxy. Applied via hot glue gun.

**Wood-colored epoxy:** The type of glue you'll most often use. Strong, lightweight, and long-lasting. Comes in two tubes, mixed in small amounts as needed. Follow package instructions and apply with toothpicks.

**Clear epoxy:** Also strong and long-lasting but slightly runnier than wood-colored epoxy. Comes in two parts and mixed as needed.

Whenever you are using glue, take care not to get drips on the outside of the house. Epoxy sets very quickly and is nearly impossible to remove, unlike hot glue. This is especially important when working around hinges, as you can accidentally glue your hinge shut.

**For outdoor construction:**

There are eco-glues that can be used for certain applications, but drying time is so long that I generally avoid it, if possible.

**Birch bark samples.**

Because I am blessed to live in an area where birch trees are abundant, it is one of my most commonly used building materials. I love working with it because it is so versatile and because it comes in a wide range of colors and textures.

***Note:***

Never collect bark off a living tree! The one exception with birch bark is if the piece is being naturally shed and is about to come away from the tree. But if the piece resists at all when you pull it, it's best to leave it alone because you can damage the tree if you pull bark off prematurely.

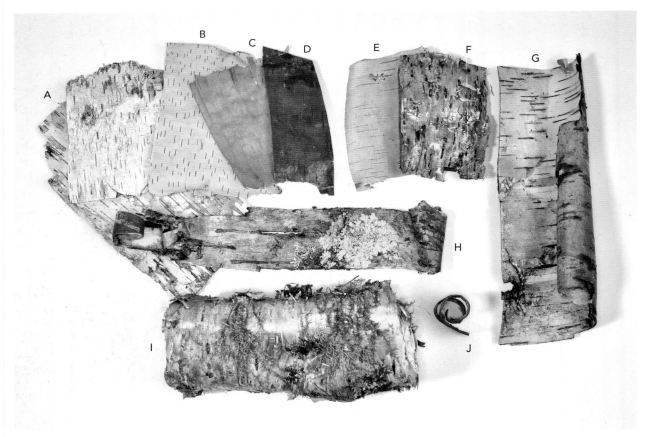

(A) Ordinary white or gray birch bark, (B–E) inner layers of white birch bark, (F) golden or yellow birch bark, (G) thick piece of white birch bark, (H) golden birch, (I) a tube of golden birch, (J) naturally occurring birch curl.

## Mushrooms and tidbits.

Below are some of my other favorite natural building materials for faerie houses, including some house elements that I would make ahead of time to take with me out into the wild to build houses that have a more finished look.

### Note:

Some of these fungi are not very durable. Use only in structures that you'll want to keep for a year or so. After that, they tend to disintegrate.

Make sure all gathered materials are brushed clean and dried fully before storing/using.

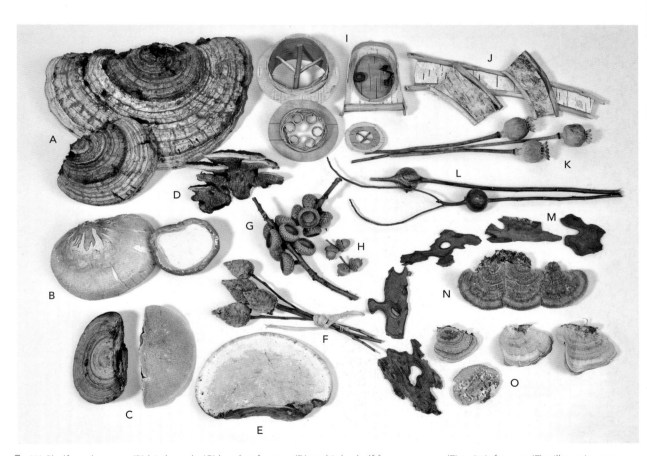

(A) Shelf mushrooms, (B) birch conk, (C) bracket fungus, (D) multiple shelf fungus group, (E) artist's fungus, (F) willow pinecone galls, (G, H) acorns, (I) premade parts for fieldwork installations, (J) premade ramps and bridge, (K) ornamental poppy pods, (L) goldenrod galls, (M) pieces of bark from red pine trees, (N, O) thin bracket fungus showing typical damage after two years of normal storage, best used for short-term projects.

## BITS AND BAUBLES FOR FINISHING TOUCHES

People often ask me where I get all of the materials that I use for decorating my houses, particularly for finishing the interiors. Because I live in a rural area, I tend to do a lot of my shopping on eBay because of the large selection and because there are international sellers with unique items. Yard sales, thrift shops, and vintage clothing (especially hats and jewelry) can have excellent potential for finding that special faerie house decoration. Etsy can be a good source as well.

Decorating these little creations is where you can really let your imagination soar. Use all kinds of materials, personalized items, and whatever bits of magic and enchantment you want to make the structure truly yours and unique. Everyone will have their own sense of style, desired color palettes, and specialty items that they want to use for their faerie houses.

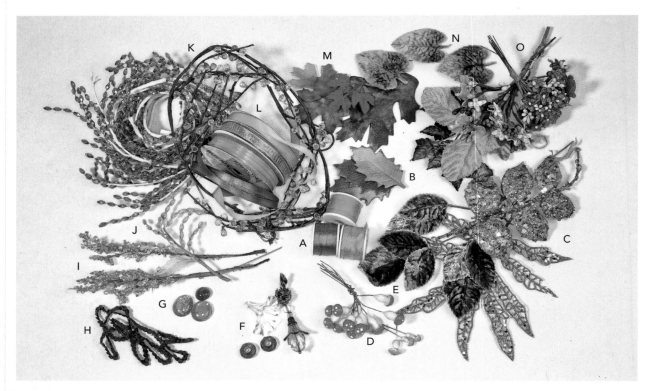

(A) Silk ribbon on spools, (B) manufactured, embossed paper leaves, (C) glittery floral embellishments, (D) miniature mushrooms made from either cotton, clay, or sculpted paper, (E) vintage velvet leaves wired together, (F) glass and acrylic beads, faceted and vintage designed beading used in lighting, (G) glass baubles, (H) sequin trim and other novelty trims, (I) glass and plastic florist accessories built onto florist wires, (J) modern beaded garlands and swags that can be taken apart, (K) vintage garlands to repurpose, (L) loose ribbons, (M) silk fabric leaves, (N) modern single velvet leaves (not wired together), (O) silk botanicals, including flowers and leaves.

Keep scale in mind and don't be afraid to take items apart in order to get at smaller components. For example, large silk flowers cut apart for their petals, sewn together, and stuffed make excellent faerie seat cushions.

Be thoughtful about the longevity of the items that you select for adding details. While feathers and butterfly wings may be appealing now, will they still look good in a year or two? It's still possible to use fragile and short-lived items in your constructions, but make sure that they are easy to repair and replace if you must use them. See page 50 for materials I commonly use for finishing touches.

Handmade mulberry and bamboo papers.

## WALL COVERINGS

There are various types of paper, wallpaper, and card stock that work well as interior wall coverings for faerie houses. Here are a few examples.

Now that you've gathered your materials and planned your house, you're ready to build!

Japanese Chiyogami papers, which make a beautiful and elegant wall-coverings.

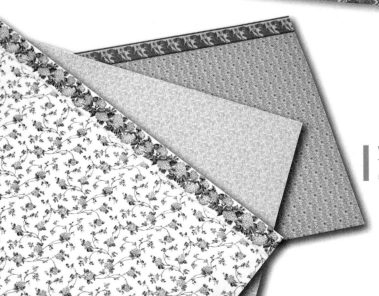

Wallpaper that is specifically made for dollhouses. The tiny delicate patterns are the perfect scale for most faerie house constructions.

# CHAPTER 3

# itty Bitty Nitty Gritty

## CREATING MAGICAL FAERIE HOUSE COMPONENTS

The magical Dragon Castle faerie house. Each roof is removable to allow viewing the exotic interior spaces. There is even a secret entrance to a crystal-lined cave under the castle for sleepy dragons to enter for a nap.

W hy do we so love the faerie world? Is it because faerie houses speak to our love of miniature things—tiny worlds where our imaginations can soar and fly? Or do we long for a place to escape? Who knows—but perhaps rather than trying to analyze it, we should just dive in and experience the simple joy of making something magical, by hand, which comes from our hearts and the materials that nature so kindly provides.

As mentioned in Chapter 2, once we have a vision and plan for the house we want to build, we begin by constructing the smaller elements first. Let's start then with an in-depth look at some of these components.

## DOORS

Most doors on human-designed houses are basic rectangles, and the same goes for windows. One of the quickest ways to make your faerie house charming and magical is literally to go outside of the box and make windows and doors that are anything but linear squares or rectangles. This simple design choice makes a huge difference. Let the shape and form of the materials guide your construction design, and your faerie house will look more natural.

Doors that open and close add a lot of interest and magic to a tiny house, but doors that are fixed in place can also be quite alluring. Because doors and windows are made at such a small scale with many fine details such as hinges, doorknobs, latticework, etc., it's much easier create these separately and then attach them to the main house.

The initial factor to consider when designing the door is whether the house has flat walls or curved walls. It is far easier to make a flat door than a curved one, but the challenge becomes how to attach a flat door to a curved wall and have a nice "fit" over the opening. You can solve that problem by creating a special vestibule entrance that has a flat front to support the flat door with curved edges on the back to accommodate the curved wall of the house. You will still make doors for flat-walled houses ahead of time, but the whole process is much easier with flat walls.

Don't worry, this will all make sense as we go along!

If you've never made a faerie house before, you might want your first house to have a fixed-in-place door. If you have some crafting skills already and really like the idea of a door that opens and closes, then you may want to skip ahead and try your hand at crafting a hinged design.

Let me share some examples of what I'm talking about to make it easier to appreciate the different options.

## FIXED, CLOSED DOORS ON FLAT WALLS WITH VESTIBULES AND SURROUNDS

Opposite are four examples of fixed, closed doors installed on flat walls. These doors do not open but, as you can see, it is quite possible to create an elaborate entrance design even when the door itself is reasonably basic.

Each of these doors represents the same style of function and construction method. They are made in the "fixed" position (they do not open) and they have detailed surrounds to enhance their impact and appearance.

## FIXED DOORS ON CURVED WALLS

Because many faerie houses are constructed with curved walls, it is helpful to know how to insert a flat door and have it look good. Usually, the trick is to float the door in a frame or vestibule within the curved wall. As shown here, this can work beautifully.

This door is flat and the wall has a gentle curve to it, but because the door is set into a deep frame, the flat door can rest in the curved surface of the wall without difficulty.

This door is attached to a curved wall but is fixed in the open position—a good solution to the flat door/curved wall problem.

## HINGED DOORS

Here are some examples of simple hinged doors. If you don't plan to handle the door a great deal, one nice way to make hinges is to use tiny silk leaves or simple ribbons, which allow the door to swing a bit. This is a good technique for especially tiny doors.

ABOVE: This tiny, 1"–wide door swings on tiny silk ribbons that you can see just on the right side of the door.

RIGHT: This rather simple door has wire hinges. One of the features that makes this door so inviting is the glass "leaf" bead, which forms a window in the door. Additionally, you can see that the twig that forms part of the frame is the same twig upon which the door is hung—another simple, elegant solution.

*All* hinged doors should always swing *out* from a faerie house. If they swing inward, then it is sometimes difficult for human-sized hands to get inside the small doorway to pull the door closed!

## HINGED DOORS WITH ELABORATE SURROUNDS

Once you feel confident in your building skills, you can get more creative with the details surrounding the door. Here are some examples of doors that move on wire hinges with embellishments in the framing surrounding the door.

### LET YOUR IMAGINATION SOAR!

These images should help you see some of what is possible in making magical faerie house doors. As with all things, if you're new to faerie house design and construction, it is best to begin learning by first working with simpler designs. As your skills improve, you can expand your construction dreams.

## "STAINED GLASS" DOORS

For the most exotic doors and entryways one can take things a step further and make doors that are transparent or translucent. They are difficult to make, so they are not covered in this book but are included for inspiration. They are made, in part, using photos of dragonfly wings printed on acetate, which creates the filigree pattern that you see.

The enchanting quality of these "stained glass" doors is really seen at their best when twilight descends and the lights in the faerie house get switched on.

# HOW TO BUILD A
# TWIG-FRAMED FIXED DOOR WITH A SIMPLE SURROUND

Whether your faerie house will have round walls or flat walls, it is easiest to make your door as part of a larger vestibule that you will then attach to the house. I like to let the materials guide the shape of the door, so to speak. We will eventually add this to our Green Dreams House (detailed in Chapter 6).

## MATERIALS

Flat piece of birch bark or smooth bark for flat wall of vestibule

Contrasting piece of birch bark or smooth bark for the door front

Two strips of birch bark or smooth bark for the arched roof of the vestibule around the door

Twigs to frame the door

Bead or other suitable material for doorknob

Fine-gauge wire

Wood-colored epoxy glue

Hot glue sticks

## TOOLS

Scissors

Fine-tipped pruners

Wire snips

Hot glue gun

Toothpicks
(to apply epoxy glue)

Fine-toothed flat saw

A fixed door in a vestibule.

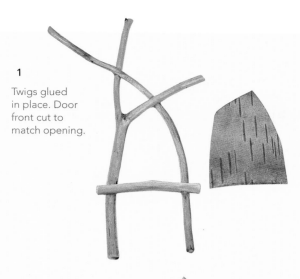

**1**

Twigs glued
in place. Door
front cut to
match opening.

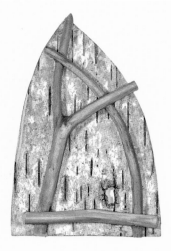

**2**

Trimmed twigs
to match the
vestibule wall.

**3**

Back view of
the door being
glued in place.

**4**

Applying the
doorknob bead.

## STEP I

Lay out the twigs that will frame the door. Use overlapping
and underlapping joints, if possible. Trim and carve the
twigs Lincoln Log–style to get the twigs to lie as flat as
possible. Use wood-colored epoxy to glue twigs together.

Cut a door from a contrasting piece of birch bark. Make
the door a tiny bit larger than the opening in the frame.
*Do not* attach yet.

## STEP 2

Cut out the large flat piece of birch bark into an arched
shape for the vestibule face wall. The arch can be
symmetrical or asymmetrical, but it should extend a bit
beyond all the glued joints of the twig frame. Using a fine-
toothed flat saw, trim the ends of the twigs so that the frame
now fits perfectly inside the vestibule wall panel.

## STEP 3

Trim the piece of bark you're using for the door front so that
none of it shows beyond the frame edge and use epoxy
glue to attach it to the twig frame. You can use tiny dots of
hot glue to temporarily hold the door in the proper place
within the frame while you apply the epoxy.

## STEP 4

To attach the doorknob, run a thin wire through the bead
and then bend it so the wire forms a horseshoe shape.
Pierce a small hole in the door for each wire and insert the
wires through the holes. Bend the wires flat on the back side
of the door and epoxy-glue the wires down so the bead
cannot be pulled out. You can use the same method for
anchoring seeds, shells, jewelry findings, or any sort of item
you want to use for a doorknob. ***Note:*** *Be very careful doing
this step because thin bark can tear easily.*

**5**

The framed door glued to the vestibule wall.

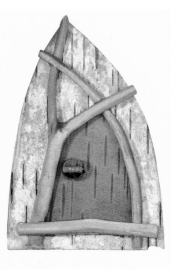

## STEP 5

Carefully center the frame on the wall and glue the door and frame assembly to the vestibule wall. Quickly remove any visible epoxy glue before it hardens.

## STEP 6

Cut two strips of birch bark that will form the arched roof of the vestibule. The strips should be the same width as each other and the lengths should match the length of the arched edge of the wall. You want bark that is fairly sturdy yet flexible enough to wrap smoothly along the side of the wall. If you have bark that is naturally curved already, this is ideal to use.

**6**

Two strips cut to form the roof.

## STEP 7

Glue the roof strips to the wall panel, positioning the wall panel along the center of the strip. Starting at the top of the arch, hold the strip of bark against the wall panel and apply three to five small drops of hot glue to hold the strip in place. Do not put the hot glue at the very beginning or at the very end of the strip. You want these joints to be filled only with the epoxy. Once the hot glue drops have set, fill in the entire back side of the joint with epoxy glue.

When the second strip is glued in place and is solid, fill in the apex of the arch on the back side with an extra bit of epoxy glue. Apply a thin bead of epoxy glue to the apex on the front side using a sharpened toothpick.

If you desire, cut a small section of extra twig and glue it on the inside of the front apex of the arch. This adds strength to that joint and hides the place where the two strips come together.

Congratulations, your door is finished!

**7**

Three dots of hot glue and four sections of epoxy glue on the arch, back view.

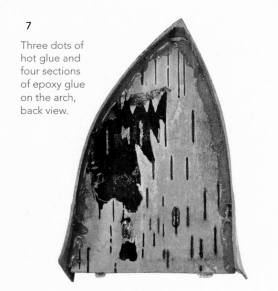

The finished door and vestibule with a peg at the apex of the arch.

Here is an example of a door made using the same technique.

# HOW TO BUILD A
# HINGED DOOR IN AN ARCHED FRAME

The movement of hinged doors adds an extra bit of magic to faerie houses. This door will eventually find a home in our Golden Cottage house, built in Chapter 6. You can use the techniques presented in this tutorial to create other types of hinged doors.

## MATERIALS

Small twigs

Arched loop of padded florist's wire

Thin birch bark or other thin bark

Medium-thick birch bark

Dark or contrasting birch bark, bark, or card stock for door front

Raffia

Very fine plastic-coated aluminum wire (used in jewelry making)

Bead or other feature for doorknob

Hot glue

Wood-colored epoxy glue

Jeweler's head pin (soft wire with a bead/head on one end)

Piece of paper

## TOOLS

Tweezers

Hot glue gun

Wire snips

Pencil

Sandpaper

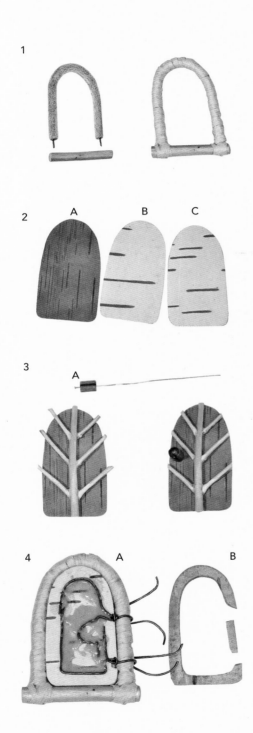

## STEP 1

Make the door arch using the padded florist's wire. Cut a small twig a little bit longer than the width of the bent arch. Glue the twig to the arch using epoxy glue. Wrap the entire arch structure with the raffia strands for a smooth, natural look. On the back side, secure the ends of the raffia carefully with epoxy glue.

## STEP 2

Trace the space within the arch frame on a piece of paper to make a template for cutting the birch bark. The door should rest within the frame but not be able to be pushed through the frame. Once you have the paper pattern for your door, cut out one piece of the dark brown bark (A) for the front of the door and a second piece of thin, light-colored birch bark for the back of the door (B). If your arch is not symmetrical, be careful to make sure that the back piece is the mirror of the door front. Cut a third piece out of slightly thicker bark for the inner middle layer (C). Once you have this middle layer piece cut out, trim a very tiny amount off all around the entire piece so that it is just barely smaller than the door front and back.

## STEP 3

Carefully cut small twigs so that they fit together in a leaf vein pattern. The twig pattern, when laid out, should be larger than the door front. Using fine sandpaper, sand the twigs so they fit nicely on the vertical stem. Use tiny drops of wood-colored epoxy to attach the angled twigs onto the central stem.

Using small beads of wood-colored epoxy, attach the twig assembly to the front of the door making sure that the "stem" is flush with the bottom of the door front and that the small "branches" extend beyond the edge of the door. Let dry until the glue is firm. Prepare the doorknob bead (A) by inserting a jeweler's head pin wire. Create a tiny hole in the door front and feed the wire through the hole, bend the wire over, and glue it down with epoxy.

## STEP 4

Place the thin birch bark door back (the part without the twigs) in the arch. Determine where the hinges should go and cut small notches for the wire. Cut small pieces of wire and bend as shown (A). Make sure that the wire is at least ³⁄₁₆ inches away from all the edges of the door back. When you have the wires where you want them, use a thin amount of wood-colored epoxy to glue in place.

Cut out a narrow band of the trimmed middle layer, as shown (B). This will go around the outside of the wire that you just glued onto the door back. Cut an additional small vertical piece to go in the space between the hinges (Figure B).

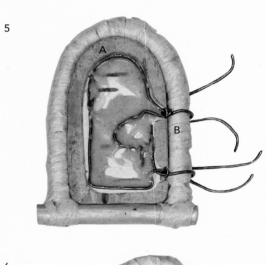

## STEP 5

Carefully glue the C-shaped piece of thick bark (A) onto the door back with epoxy glue. Also attach the small vertical piece that goes in between the hinges. (B) *Be careful not to get any epoxy on the doorframe or in the hinges, as you can accidentally glue the door shut at this stage.*

## STEP 6

On the door front panel *carefully* cut and trim off the excess twigs so that the cut ends exactly match the edge of the brown door. Use fine sandpaper to finish these twig ends nicely.

Apply a generous amount of glue to the back of the brown door front and place that on top of the door back that is sitting within the door frame arch that was just completed in the previous step, again making sure no glue leaks out. The door will now move freely within the frame. Let the entire piece dry for at least 12 hours.

Once the door is completely hard and dry, carefully trim and sand the edge of the door so that it fits nicely within the arch frame.

## STEP 7

Push the door into the closed position and bring the two unused wires from each hinge forward around the door arch frame to the front of the door. With each wire, make a decorative spiral and lay flat on the door front. Mix up a small amount of clear epoxy glue and drop a couple of drops in the center of each spiral and work the glue outwards along the wires so that the whole spiral is now glued down. Lay the door flat until the glue is completely dry. *Do not let any glue run into the hinge.* Install spacers on the outside of the door arch. Make three tiny spacers (A) from the same thick bark that was used for the middle layer of the door.

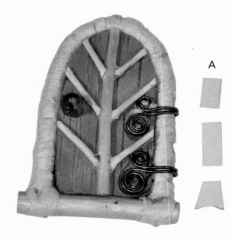

8

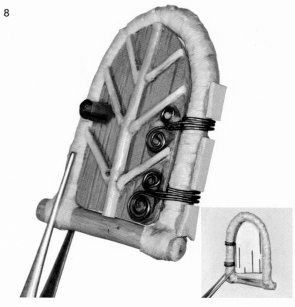

## STEP 8

Attach the spacers to the door arch in-between, above, and below the hinges. Use a thin application of wood-colored epoxy and make sure that all of the spacers lie flat in the same plane. The easiest way to do this is to press the arch against a flat surface briefly just before the glue starts to set up. *Once again, be careful about not allowing any epoxy glue to get onto the hinges or they will no longer work properly.*

## STEP 9

Cut the strip of nice birch bark that you have left into an awning. Hold it up around the door to get the right shape.

## STEP 10

Once the awning strip has been trimmed and shaped properly, use a thin amount of epoxy glue to attach the awning to the arch, again avoiding getting any glue on the hinges.

Congratulations! You have a finished hinged door.

9

10

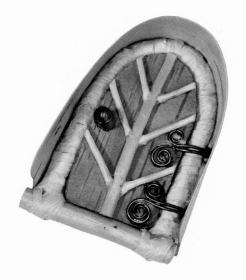

Here are some other examples of doors that were created using similar techniques. Note how there is an upright twig in each example to support the hinges. This works really well and is easy to make.

A simple hinged door.

This doorknob is an earring! Cut tiny channels in the upright supports for the hinge wires to ensure that the door does not slide down the twig over time and with use. Use a folded-over piece of fine sandpaper to make this groove if the twig is small and delicate.

OPPOSITE: A grapevine decoration is sewn to the door's front panel before being glued onto the full door.

## WINDOWS

In simplest terms, a window is an opening between the inner house and outer world. Other than the door, they are the most essential elements that add style and interest to the faerie house.

Once you know the basic configuration for your faerie house, it's important to decide the best location for the windows. Make sure they're in scale with the door and other basic aspects of the house. If you make your windows too small, they will be difficult to create. If the windows are too large, the walls of the house may become too flimsy.

Other things to think about include what you want for glazing material. (Cellophane films are available at craft stores.) Think about whether you want curtains and whether you'll want to add lighting. Do you want to make simple yet charming windows, or do you want to make something extravagant with lots of detail?

If you're going to have multiple windows, it's best to use a similar design style for all of the windows so that the whole house has a pleasing and harmonious appearance.

### GENERAL INSTRUCTIONS FOR BUILDING WINDOWS

1. Decide on the relative size and placement of windows for the house. I usually make paper patterns or templates for each separate window.
2. Cut the opening in the wall of the house to create the opening for the window.
3. Install the window either by applying a decorative frame with some sort of nice finish to the opening so that the raw cut edge is hidden from view or insert a complete window that has been fabricated ahead of time for the corresponding opening in the house.
4. Finish with a frame on the outside and/or inside to hide raw construction edges.

### WINDOW STYLES

Because there are so many options for window designs and techniques, let's break it down and examine different examples of the kinds of windows you might want to make for your house.

**Flat-Frame Style Windows.**

Flat-framed windows are the easiest to make and are a good place to begin. They can be round, oval, parabolic, arched, or any unusual shape you desire, as they're usually just a simple opening cut in the wall with a simple frame to surround the opening. The trick to successfully making flat-framed windows is to ensure that the surrounding frame covers the edge of the cut window opening. Use twigs and other fine materials to add details to the windows and frames.

Here are some examples.

Flat-framed windows are great to make ahead of time in pairs or sets for adding to faerie houses you may want to make out in the wild. If you plan to leave your faerie house structure in the woods, then it is best to use non-toxic, non-plastic adhesives to construct your windows so that they will decompose as naturally as possible.

**Twig-Framed Windows.**

These windows are very similar to the flat-framed style except that rather than using flat bark to frame the window, you'll use twigs, which determine the shape of the window. Always select your twigs first and make the window frame before cutting the window opening in the wall of the house. That way they will match.

Because twigs are generally straight or flat when laid on a surface, these windows are best suited for flat wall construction. Trying to make the twig frame go around a curved wall is difficult and not recommended unless you are skillful or have access to a lot of curved twigs.

## Porthole Windows.

Porthole windows are similar to flat-framed windows but have an additional strip of material that is used to line the opening of the window. This becomes an important element of the window construction and design. I use porthole window construction a lot because it is a great way to install a window in a curved surface. The porthole window usually sticks out a fair amount from the curved wall and offers a design element that looks a bit like an awning for the inserted window. This inner liner/awning then needs an outside frame, which is very similar to the first design style, the flat-framed window.

Porthole windows can have any sort of mullion or divider used to divide the interior space of the window just as with the flat-framed windows.

## MULLION DETAILS

Mullions are the additional delicate elements within the frame of the windows that add style and interest. The important thing to keep in mind is to stay to scale and to make sure that whatever you use for mullions is firmly attached to the frame of the window on the inside. Here are some examples.

**Latticework.**

Latticework can be done with fine twigs, thin strips of birch bark, hemp, or linen twine. It is usually not necessary to actually weave the lattice together as this is too difficult for most of these small spaces.

**Unusual Mullion Examples.**
Unusual mullions can be made by creatively manipulating fine botanical materials. In this example, a single weeping willow branch was twisted upon itself several times to create the delicate mullion within the circular frame. Notice the freshly harvested hazel leaf draperies that I placed inside the window before setting the entire window assembly into the moss wall.

Twig mullions in a door window.

## BAY WINDOWS

Add a bay window for extra interest. These are basically tiny half-rooms with a prominently featured window stuck onto the side wall of a house. Bay windows are generally curved and need a roof and some sort of support to attach the rounded space to the main house. Bay windows bulge out from a wall with brackets or corbel supports below the window to anchor it to the main house. Let's look at some.

## WINDOWS IN STONE HOUSES

Stone-walled faerie houses are always magical, but without windows and doors they look more like fortifications. Adding a door vestibule and windows to the stone portions of a tiny house make the whole structure more inviting and interesting. However, if you are building a dry-laid house outdoors, without mortar, then you must be very careful to make sure your wall will not become weak by opening it up for a window. In such cases, a single window (below) may be a better option.

ABOVE: Windows that will be incorporated into stone structures are made separately and added to the walls as they are raised.

RIGHT: It is best to use minimal to no glue in windows for stone houses that will be left to weather the elements. This window is made from several green braches from a nearby weeping willow tree.

ABOVE: I made the door and windows for this house in the studio using eco-glue and then brought them to the site where the house was built.

RIGHT: These arch-shaped windows were made ahead of time and then placed in the wall as it was being built. Each window assembly consists of the curved twig (that was bent and dried months before), a matching straight sill twig that has been glued to the arch, a lattice of toothpicks, and sturdy birch bark liners that match the arch and project back into the full thickness of the walls. I used toothpicks so that the delicate open fronts would be strong and keep their shape under the weight of the stones above.

## WINDOWS WITH LIGHTING

Windows are especially enchanting if your house has lighting built into the structure. You can light the faerie house by installing small, battery-powered lights.

A single battery-powered tea light makes this house glow.

Micro LED lights illuminate this house.

Sometimes lighting is configured so both the inside and the outside of the house are illuminated using a single strand of lights.

Windows are one of the biggest design features on a faerie house. Start out with the simpler styles and get used to how they are made. Then let your skills grow along with your imagination as you tackle more elaborate and challenging designs.

In the tutorials that follow, I will show you some basic and simple techniques to give you a good start in seeing how these little elements are fabricated. Some of the windows demonstrated in these tutorials will be used later in Chapter 6.

# HOW TO MAKE A
# FLAT-FRAMED WINDOW

Flat-framed windows are some of the easiest window styles to make, and they can be made in almost any shape that you wish. For this tutorial, we will make a triangular window for a round-walled house that will eventually end up in our Green Dreams House, detailed in Chapter 6. However, you can use these techniques to make any framed window for a flat- or curved-wall house.

## MATERIALS

Two identical pieces of contrasting birch bark (or thin material that will contrast with the material used for the outer covering of the house) cut into frames for the window

One long narrow strip of birch bark (or thin, flexible material) for the liner of the window

Sapphire faerie film (a thin, transparent material with a reflective surface)

Wood-colored epoxy glue

Glue sticks

## TOOLS

X-Acto knife

Scissors

Pencil

Tweezers

Hot glue gun

A finished flat-framed window.

CHAPTER 3

## STEP 1

Using one of the window frames as a template, carefully trace an outline of the inner opening of the window onto the main body of the house. Make this line as faint as possible but still visible. Carefully using a very sharp X-Acto knife, cut out the window opening. Make your cut on the outside of the line you drew so that the actual window opening will be just slightly (about 1mm) larger than the opening in the frame that you used for a template. That way, once the frame is installed, you'll see the inside edge of the frame rather than the raw edge of the opening cut into the wall. Use the side of the tip of the hot glue gun and sear the edge of the cut opening. This helps smooth the cut edge. No glue is applied.

## STEP 2

Cut the transparent film so that it is slightly smaller than the outside edge of the window frame.

## STEP 3

Use wood-colored epoxy glue to affix the window frame over the cut opening in the house. Take care to ensure no glue appears on the front side. Take the long thin strip of birch bark (A) and gently fold it so that it completely fills the window frame. You may need to use a small tweezers to hold and coax the liner strip all the way into all the corners. Carefully glue the strip in place from the inside of the house using wood-colored epoxy glue, keeping the liner edge flush with the inside of the wall. It usually helps to have the liner strip overlap itself along the bottom edge so that the windowsill is reinforced with the two layers of the liner.

## STEP 4

From the inside, apply hot glue sparingly to the inside wall of the house and affix the transparent film centered over the window opening. Test the interior window frame in place and make sure no film edges stick out from behind the frame. Trim glazing material if needed, and then glue the frame in place over the film to create a finished interior look.

1

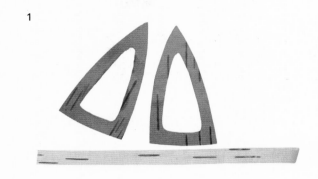

2

3

A

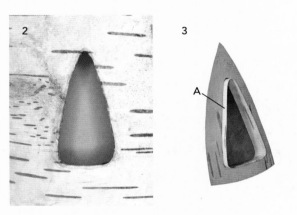

4

Here are some other examples of windows that are made using the same basic principles in this tutorial.

# HOW TO MAKE A
# WINDOW WITH A FRAME WITHIN A LINER

This kind of window can be made for either a curved or flat wall. I will demonstrate on a flat wall, but the same steps are done for installation in a curved wall, the main difference being that you'll need to make sure that the tube/liner that the frame sits within is a little deeper so you'll have enough depth to accommodate the curved wall. If that sounds confusing, check out the porthole window tutorial and you'll see how it would work with a curved wall. This window will eventually end up in our Golden Cottage house.

## MATERIALS

Thin twigs

Rigid material for window frames; can be medium-weight birch bark, matboard, very heavy paper, etc.

Flexible, thin bark for the window liner (can also use heavy paper)

Hot glue sticks

Wood-colored epoxy glue

Piece of paper for making a pattern

## TOOLS

Tweezers

X-Acto knife

Hot glue gun

Pencil

Sandpaper

Scissors

A finished window.

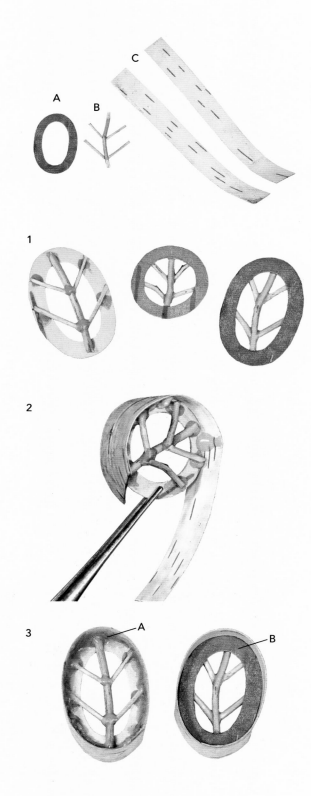

To make these windows, you will need an oval frame made from semi-stiff material such as birch bark (used here). Matboard or stiff decorative paper will also work (A). Be choosy about this piece. The bark should be the kind that does not delaminate (peel and come apart) easily. It should be thick enough to flex slightly, but rigid enough to stay flat as you build the window. I've used twig mullions (B) here but the windows can be open, glazed, or made using any sort of material you'd like for the interior of the window. A butterfly wing or silk flower petal covering half of the open window would make a lovely curtain-like effect.

You'll also need a flexible strip of clean birch bark (C) or heavy paper for the lining. The strip should be long enough to go around the frame with a little overlap and should be as wide as you want the window to be deep with a little extra width for good measure. You will need a frame, twig mullion, and liner for one window. Multiply the materials for the number of windows desired.

## STEP 1

Build the mullions within the frame. Carefully trim twigs and glue them together to form a leaf-vein patterned mullion. Once the glue is lightly set, you can glue the mullions to the backs of the window frames. Then trim away excess glue visible from the front. Let dry completely before going to the next step.

## STEP 2

Hold the window frame with tweezers. Begin gluing the liner strip to the edge of the frame. Anchor the strip to the frame with a tiny drop of hot glue on the inside of the window (the side that will face inside the house). Roll the frame a quarter turn while wrapping the strip tight against the frame edge. Apply another tiny drop of hot glue to hold the strip in place. Turn another quarter turn and repeat. Do this until the entire frame has been wrapped with the strip. Trim off the excess at the overlap. Glue the overlap with epoxy glue, not hot glue.

## STEP 3

Carefully apply wood-colored epoxy all around the inside of the frame where it joins up with the liner strip (A). Make sure none of the epoxy shows from the front side. This will reinforce the small hot glue dots that anchored the liner strip in place. Install the liner strip (B).

## STEP 4

Place the window on a piece of paper and trace around it. This will serve as your template to cut the opening for the window in the wall of the house. Cut an opening in the paper using the traced line. Test the paper template by gently pushing your window into the opening of the paper. Do not force it; it should just barely fit.

4

## INSTALLING THE WINDOWS

Take the paper template and position it over the place where you want your window to be in your faerie house. Hold the paper and carefully trace a pencil line onto your wall material. Using a sharp X-Acto knife, cut along the pencil line or a little to the inside of the line to make the opening in your wall. It is best to cut it a little small and sand the opening with sandpaper to make the final fit adjustments. Place the window into the opening in the wall. Use sandpaper along the edges to adjust the opening until your window fits perfectly. From the back side (interior side), use wood-colored epoxy glue to attach the window to the wall opening.

Congratulations! You've made and installed a beautiful window!

Following are some other examples of windows made using the same technique.

# HOW TO MAKE A
# PORTHOLE WINDOW

Porthole windows are an excellent choice when working with curved- or round-walled structures. They provide an elegant solution to a difficult problem: how to make a window that curves. You'll make these windows using a combination of techniques used for flat-framed windows and framed windows within a liner, so it is a good idea to practice with those first if you are new to window constructing.

Your finished windows will add a lot of charm to your faerie house, in addition to structural integrity from the epoxy glue. Experiment with different shapes once you have the skills. The frame itself can be shaped, decorated, or have contrasting and multiple layers. Silk flower petals, moss, beads, and so forth can be applied to the top of the porthole liner/awning for additional color and texture.

## MATERIALS

Twigs (if you want
twig mullions)

Birch bark, heavy paper,
or another smooth
flexible material

Tube of birch bark to simulate
a round or circular house

Wood-colored epoxy glue

Hot glue sticks

## TOOLS

Tweezers

Hot glue gun

Scissors

Paper

Pencil

X-Acto knife

A porthole window installed in a birch bark wall.

## STEP 1

Make a window template from a piece of paper that is the shape and size you want. Use this template to cut a hole in the wall of the faerie house that matches the template exactly. Save the template. Cut a window frame (A) using the template. This frame will hold the porthole liner and will be affixed to the outside wall of the house. The inner opening of the frame should be a tiny bit smaller than the template line, and the outside edge of the frame needs to be larger than the template line. This will ensure that the frame will correctly cover the opening in the wall.

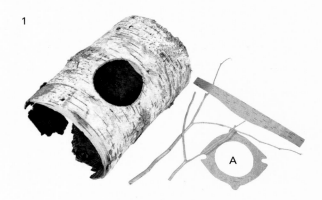

## STEP 2

Form the long strip of birch bark into a circle and insert it into the opening of the frame. You may need to apply a tiny dot of hot glue just to temporarily hold it in place. It should fit snugly but still allow for adjustment between the frame and the wall of the house. The joint of the strip should be positioned at the bottom of the window once it is assembled.

Insert the window assembly into the opening in the faerie house wall and gently re-position the frame so that it closely matches the curve of the house wall while the liner has full contact all around the window opening.

Carefully remove the window assembly from the house, making sure it does not move and apply four dots of hot glue to anchor the curved frame onto the liner. Re-test the alignment in the opening of the house wall.

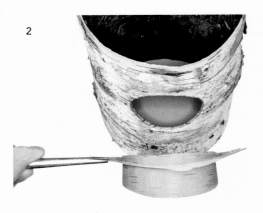

## STEP 3

If all is well, remove the assembly and glue the frame to the liner tube on the *back* side using wood-colored epoxy. Start by gluing the top half of the liner to the window frame first. Let dry. Next, glue the overlapping junction of the liner itself. You need to do this to give that part of the window extra strength. Finally, glue the lower half of the liner into the frame. It is best to work slowly.

If you've done it correctly, no glue will show from the outside of the window assembly. The window is now ready to install into the house if no mullions are desired. If you wish, add curtains (silk flower petals, leaves, ribbons, etc.) or glazing material (faerie film, sheet mica) to the back of the window after you install it into the house.

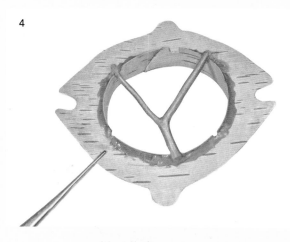

4

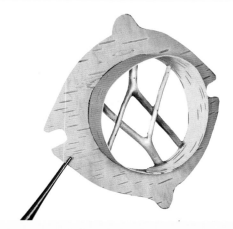

5

6

## STEP 4 (optional)

Turn the window assembly so that the inside of the frame is facing upward and test your twig arrangement on the opening to get the design you want. Trim the twigs so they are just barely longer than the opening of the window. You may want to cut small notches in the liner to hold the ends of the twigs in the proper placement. Use wood-colored epoxy to glue the twigs in place, making sure to keep the inside of the window opening free from any glue drips.

## STEP 5 (optional)

If you are creating a lattice-like mullion, apply one layer first, let dry and then apply the second layer of twigs. Don't try to do it all at once because the twigs sometimes move when you clean up the excess glue.

## STEP 6 (optional)

Install the window in the house. Insert the entire assembly into the opening of the wall and test the position. Be sure that the overlapping junction on the liner is positioned at the bottom of your window. Remove the window assembly. Apply epoxy to the back of the entire frame and reinsert the window assembly into the opening in the wall. Hold it in place until it is set.

## STEP 7 (optional)

You can add more glue to the inside of the window if you want a perfect seal. Just make sure that the extra glue goes in the space between the window liner and the original opening that was cut in the wall.

The finished porthole window in a curved wall.

Here are some other examples of porthole-style windows.

# HOW TO BUILD A
# BAY WINDOW

Bay windows make wonderful additions to faerie houses. They can be added to just about any structure with a little planning and care. This tutorial will show you how to make a basic bay window on a flat-walled structure. Once you have mastered this technique, you can adapt the process in a variety of ways for your faerie house creations.

Two questions influence where I choose to place a bay window:

1. Is there enough space on the house itself so it can be sufficiently anchored to the wall of the house without looking clumsy or being structurally deficient?
2. Will this structure enhance or detract from the overall design?

## MATERIALS

Twigs (if you want twig mullions)

Birch bark, heavy paper, or another smooth flexible material in at least two contrasting colors

Wood-colored epoxy glue

Felt

Hot glue sticks

Wallpaper for interior

## TOOLS

Tweezers

Hot glue gun

Scissors

Paper

Pencil

X-Acto knife

A three-pane bay window with twig lattice. Note that the single piece of brown bark with three oval holes gives the look of three separate windows.

If the window will be an enhancement and structurally supported, then I often make a little sketch of how I want the bay window to look. Keep in mind that the roof for the bay window will be below the eaves of the house and should match stylistically. This tutorial shows how to make the bay window for the Golden Cottage featured in Chapter 6. The space was tight, so the roof for the bay window is going to be simple and have a rather low pitch or slant so it will not take up too much room.

Because the house will be finished on the inside and lighted, I will include the steps needed to prepare the window for those additions. If your house is not going to have lighting or will be unfinished on the inside, you can skip those parts of the tutorial.

## STEP 1

Cut the opening for the bay window into the house wall panel (A). The curved window panel that already has a round window installed in it (B) is the height of the opening in the house wall plus ¼ inch. Cut tiny ⅛-inch notches at each corner of the bay window panel top and bottom.

The length of the window panel is longer than the width of the opening cut in the wall so that this piece will form a bowed-out shape when the ends are placed within the opening in the main wall. A roof will be made from the curved piece of white birch bark (C). The bottom of the bowed window will be made from a similarly shaped and matching piece of golden birch bark (D).

## STEP 2

Cover the entire bowed window wall with brown felt to block out any possible light leaks around the round window. Curve the wall as you apply the felt. Cut out the notches at the corners.

## STEP 3

If you plan to finish the interior of your house, this is the time to add the wallpaper to this piece. Make your wallpaper the same shape and size as this curved window panel (B) section but attach the wallpaper *only* at the edge of the circular window. Leave the rest unattached to the wall section for the moment.

In addition, use the main house wall panel (A) as a template and cut out a matching piece of wallpaper. Cut out the opening in the wallpaper just as the opening is in the wall panel (A). Set aside.

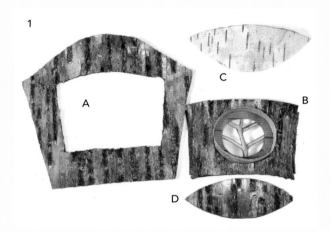

## STEP 4

Insert the curved window panel into the house wall, making sure that the round window is right side up. The curved wall should fit snugly into place. Tack into position with four dots of hot glue from the inside. Do not put the hot glue at the exact corner as this needs to be glued well with the epoxy glue. On the inside, glue this joint well with wood-colored epoxy all along the entire X–Y length of both ends.

## STEP 5

When the epoxy is solidly set, create a paper pattern for both the roof and the base. Make your adjustments to the paper pattern until you are satisfied, then cut out the good materials you will use for the roof and the bottom. Make wallpaper copies of the roof and base. Do not install these pieces yet. Turn the house wall panel over and work on the inside. Using hot glue, attach the wallpaper pieces to the inside of the bay window as shown. You may need to add extra strips of paper to cover all the joins. Each window is different, so work slowly and finesse each piece into place.

## STEP 6

Once the bowed window well has been wallpapered, secure the round window frame in place with epoxy glue. Then apply the full wall piece of wallpaper to the wall of the house. This will cover over any of the raw edges of wallpaper and give a clean finish to the inside of the bay window.

The wall with window should look like this from the inside (A); and from the outside (B).

If you plan on lighting the house, I recommend covering the back side of the exposed wallpaper with felt before attaching the roof and base of the bay window.

4

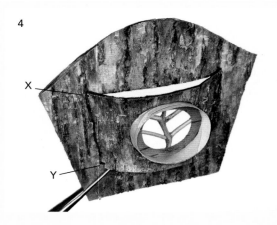

5

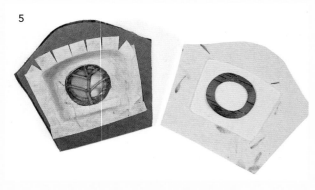

6

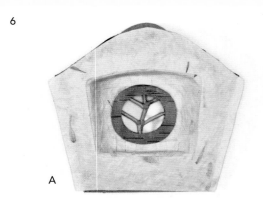

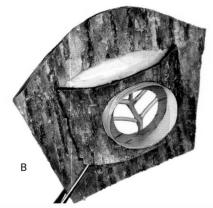

## STEP 7

Attach the roof/awning. Apply the glue to the top edge of the roof and the top edge of the curved wall for cleanest results. Use epoxy glue and be careful not to leave any drips. Hold the roof in place while the glue sets. Be sure to have extra glue in the corners for a solid joint.

## STEP 8

Now glue the bottom carefully in place using the same process.

7

8

Sometimes, if I know in advance that the roof is going to be a challenge to apply, I attach the wallpaper *after* I have added the roof so I have access to these critical joints and can glue them well.

## HIDE AND STRENGTHEN

One good way to camouflage the joints is to add twig or silk leaf details over the place where the curved piece meets the main house. This is a good idea if the house is particularly delicate.

Twigs hide construction joints in several places on this house.

## BAY WINDOW, *continued*

If you plan on making an upholstered window seat inside the house, you can do that now. It is much easier to work in this tiny area while it is separate from the house. Once the main house is all put together, it is sometimes hard to reach these little nooks.

Here are two examples of window seats made in bay-type windows.

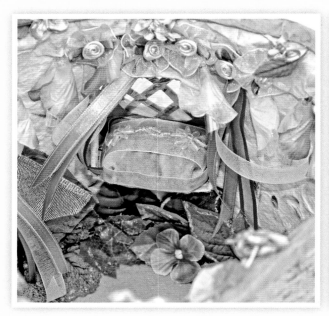

Here is a visual tutorial showing how I attached two bowed windows to a curved-wall faerie house. Now that you know how it is done, you should be able to see some extra tips in these images.

A curved-wall faerie house base with attachment cleats (A) for bay windows.

Bay windows positioned (see pages 90 to 93 for instructions on how to make bay windows).

Apply glue to the entire edge of the bay window bump-out and to the cleats and attach the bay window. Hold it in place until it is set.

The moss was gently pulled away from the main house to add the windows and was glued back in place when finished.

The finished house with the shelf-mushroom roofs applied to both bay windows, which match the main shelf-mushroom roof.

## TOWERS AND PORCHES

As you become a more experienced builder, you may wish to add a tower or porch to your house. These pieces are best constructed separately and then added onto the main structure once you have the doors and windows installed. The construction techniques for towers are similar to bay windows, except that the curve of the tower is usually more extreme and the tower is usually finished with a full roof and complete support base. Install the windows in the tower first before adding it to the house. Afterward, finish the top and bottom. To install, cut a small, narrow opening, then glue the tower directly onto the house. This is similar to the way bay windows are installed.

Here are some examples of towers.

▌ Bay window on left, tower on right.

LEFT: The tower was added above the roofline using a conical support.

BELOW: A free-standing tower (left) and bay window (right).

A tiny porch with delicate framing.

Porches are handled much the same way as bay windows, except they are usually more open structures that can be built out from the house using twig framing and don't require doors or windows. Remember to plan for a roof that complements the main house.

Now that you know how to make the most important structural details, the next step will be to work on the inside and add lighting (if desired), which we will look at in the next chapter.

A porch with a shelf fungus roof.

# adding twinkle and style

## LIGHTING AND INTERIORS

f inishing the interior of your faerie house has many advantages. The materials used will add strength and beauty to your creation, plus it's very satisfying to decorate the interiors so that viewers can see that the inside of the house is just as lovingly crafted as the outside. First, we'll look at lighting, as that is an integral part of adding sparkle and style, and then we'll continue with finishing the rest of the interior of the house.

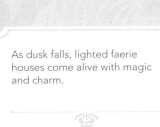

As dusk falls, lighted faerie houses come alive with magic and charm.

## LIGHTING

There's nothing quite like bringing one (or more!) of these little houses out into the garden, turning on the lights, and enjoying the enchanting glow. Faerie houses that are made with some form of lighting have an extra aura of realism.

Exterior lighting can also be welcoming.

There are several different lighting methods available. Lighting design depends primarily on whether the roof will be removable. If the roof is fixed in place and all of the lights are inside the house, then not as much detailing work needs to be done to hide the wiring or decorate the bulbs, as they will only be viewable through the windows. If the roof is removable, then more effort is made to give a finished look. All of the lighting that I install is battery-powered LED lighting because it is safe, efficient, and allows you to enjoy your house anywhere.

It takes a fair degree of patience and care to install lighting in these handmade sculptures, but the effort and time is well rewarded. Let's explore the options, tricks, and techniques.

## LIGHTING MATERIALS

No matter which form of lighting you use, you will first need to check your house with a small flashlight to make sure there are no cracks through which light will escape. You can fill cracks with epoxy, felt, patches of bark, or any other material that makes sense within the design scheme of the house.

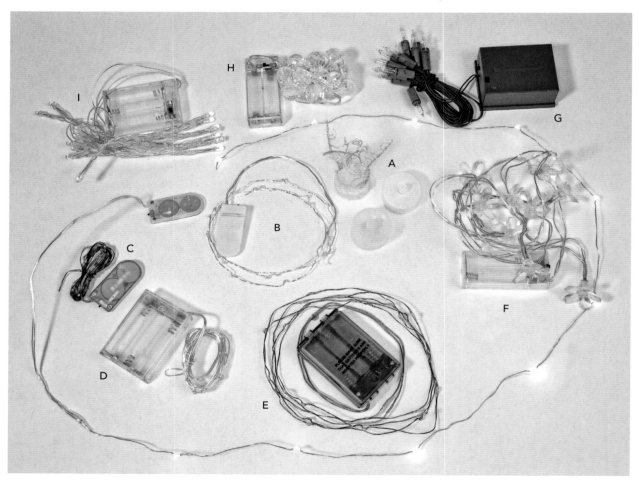

(A) Battery powered tea lights, (B, C) button battery-powered micro wire LEDs, (D, E) AA or AAA battery-powered micro LED lights, (F) AA battery-powered LED lights with acrylic flowers, (G) old-school battery-operated incandescent lights *(Note: These lights do generate a tiny bit of heat, so I generally do not recommend using them, although you can set them in the foliage around a faerie house in the garden for a nice effect)*, (H) LED lights with bare wires and bulbs encased in acrylic faceted beads, (I) LED lights that are encased in a small plastic bead and with wires covered in plastic.

A battery-powered tea light installed with fabric surrounding it to soften the glow.

## INSTALLING LIGHTING

### BATTERY-POWERED TEA LIGHTS

If you are using a battery-powered tea light, the installation process is fairly straightforward. If you have a removable roof on your faerie house, then you can simply create a place to set the tea light while it is on. Alternatively, if your house is very small, you can cut a hole in the floor just big enough to push the tea light through and glue it in place. The switch will now be accessible on the bottom of your house, and you can replace the batteries if that is an option.

### BATTERY-POWERED MICRO LED STRING LIGHTS

I most often use the ultra-thin micro wire button battery LED strings. They come in 10-, 15-, and 20-bulb strands and can be found in warm or cool white, individual colors, and mixed colors. Usually, you'll install lighting after the main structure is completed but before the interior finishing is started. This allows you to cover over the wiring after installation with wallpaper coverings.

The strings with pre-applied blossoms or beads cannot be pulled through small holes or a space narrower than the baubles. This could be a problem for some installations.

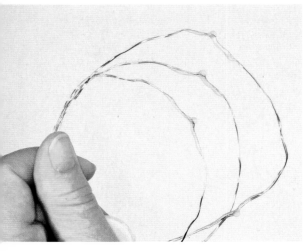

**Preparing micro LED lights for installation.**

- Apply small coatings of hot glue to both wires on either side of the LED bulb and to the back of the bulb itself. This helps protect the fragile wire from breaking during installation. It also helps to have glue pre-applied to the wire to anchor into position.

- Decide where you're going to put the battery pack before you permanently affix the lights. Make sure the pack is hidden, yet accessible, so that you can easily change the batteries and can use the switch to turn it off and on.

- Build a small holder for the battery pack out of bark, felt, or other sturdy material and secure it to the house. A good place to conceal a battery pack is under a floor with the switch access on an outside wall. Make sure you can reach the switch to operate and can pull the unit out far enough to change the batteries.

- Map out where each light is going to go. Be careful while handling the wires, as they are very fragile and can break easily. Make a tester model using string or wire with bulb placements marked on the string to map out difficult configurations. Sometimes with towers, dormers, second stories, and so forth, it is difficult to get the configuration right on the first try. Use tape to hold it in place. Do not stretch the wires as this may cause them to break.

- If there is an excessive length of wire between your chosen light placements, just make gentle *S* shapes with the wire and glue it down when you get to that part of the string.

- When the lights are in position, test the lights to make sure they work before you glue them down. Test frequently during installation. Sometimes a bulb goes dead and you have to reconfigure your lighting plan.

- If a bulb ends up being in a place where you want no light, you can mask it out by gluing a small wad of felt over the light.

Here is a birch bark box (before the lid is glued on) I made to hold the battery pack onto the house. Note the loop of wire that allows the pack to be removed completely free of the box for battery replacement. This is crucial.

## Installing micro LED lights.

Begin the installation process at the battery pack end rather than at the finished end of the string of lights. You may need to thread the light string through a tiny hole or weave it in and out of rooms, and you can't do that with the battery pack attached.

Micro LED lighting being installed.

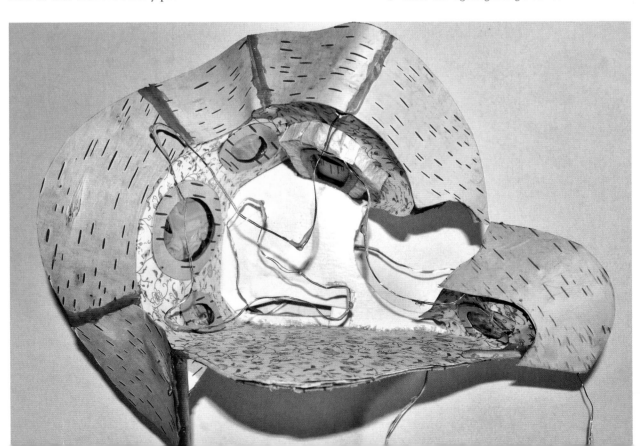

One string, two lighting styles.

Because each situation is unique, you will need to work out the best configuration for each project. Once the plan is configured, begin gluing down the wires as needed. Hot glue works very well because you can reheat it and reposition the wires if needed. Use small dots of glue to anchor everything in place first, then return and permanently attach.

If the eaves (see Chapter 5) are already in place on the house (the exposed birch bark in these images), you can simply cut a tiny hole in the eaves and just barely insert the bulb and glue it in place. This will give you a tiny light that shines down on the exterior of the house. The middle bulb in the left image has been installed using this technique.

The other two bulbs simply protrude into the room and will be covered with a large, faceted bead to act as a sconce. In this way, you can light both inside and outside using just one string of lights.

To block the light from leaking elsewhere and spoiling the effect, you'll need to apply a small patch of dark felt to the back side of eaves lights.

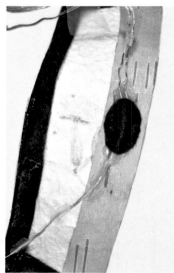

This is how the bulb looks from the outside of the house, a tiny dot emerging out of the birch bark. In this instance, the light will shine down from the eaves of the roof onto the exterior of the house. Because the LED bulbs give off no heat, it's perfectly safe to have it right next to the bark like this.

An oval pad of felt is placed over the bulb on the inside of the eaves, where it will not be seen but will serve to block any light leakage, which can spoil the lighting effect.

## Hiding the battery pack.

The battery packs for micro LED lights are small and use button batteries. They are easy to hide under foliage. You can also position them on the back of the house up near the eaves.

You can also engineer a way to have a movable leaf hide the opening if there are few other camouflage options.

Option 2

Option 1

Option 3

Before.

After.

**HIDING A LARGE BATTERY PACK.**
You'll need to get creative in hiding the larger battery pack for lights that use AA or AAA batteries. Keep in mind that the best place may be outside the house in the landscaped base.

## CAMOUFLAGING THE WIRES.

LED strings of lights are a great asset for faerie house builders, but the shiny silver wires (or other colors depending on the string you use) may not be something you want to see. Here are a couple of different ways to handle the shiny wires.

If the wires are going to be highly visible, use green or brown tissue or crepe paper to cover the wires before you install them. This turns the light string into what looks like a growing vine, which you can enhance with applied silk foliage. Narrow silk ribbon or novelty yarn works too. Apply with small amounts of hot glue so that the wires stay flexible. The opposite image shows the same structure with stair steps added and the vine lights turned on.

If you plan to wallpaper your house, you can simply paper over the wires. If you install the lighting after the wallpaper, it still may be possible to layer on matching paper. Or, if that looks messy, try using thin strips of felt or novelty yarn to simulate flower stems and add silk blossoms and leaves. Using your own creativity and decoration style, you will find many clever ways to conceal unwanted wires from view.

**Adding embellishments to lighting.**

Sometimes the bare bulb is too bright or too ordinary looking and we want to jazz things up a bit. In certain situations, hanging a glass or acrylic bead in front of the bulb works well.

Another way to make a sconce is to wrap the LED bulb in a silk petal or two. Thin, translucent petals work best.

Hanging glass leaf beads conceal bare LED bulbs, which are just emerging from the wall of the vestibule on either side of the door. The drop bead above also covers a bare LED bulb. A matching leaf-bead dangle visually ties it to the two beads below in the vestibule.

You can also use small, glittery novelty bits to add as sconce parts and decorations. It really is fun to dream up unique ways to enhance your lighting options.

Faerie houses really come to life with added lighting. Once you've mastered the basic skills, you'll have great fun making your little houses sparkle and twinkle.

The same doorway with the lights on.

Several lighting effects on one house. Notice that in the two windows the light bulbs are centered at the top of the window arch. Placing lights at either the top or the bottom of any window works better than trying to place the light in the middle of the window. The lights over the door show acrylic beads glued directly over the LED bulbs affixed with clear epoxy. Some acrylic beads may be drillable. Using beads with facets gives a sparkly look to the lighting!

In this example, the LED lights were placed around the base of the dried lotus blossom roof, and then the sparkly beaded garland with faceted beads was worked into the petals next to the lights. There is a single strand of ten lights used for this tiny (4"-tall) house—two inside and eight outside (two shining down near the door and six in the flower roof). The battery pack is hiding under the bed but accessed from outside (see movable leaf on page 109).

TOP: Fancy sconces for an elegant house.
RIGHT: Silk blossoms conceal LED lights.

## INTERIOR DECORATING

Once the body of the house is complete, you may want to decorate the interior. If the roof is fixed in place, the view of the interior will be limited, so you may want to keep the decorating to a minimum. However, if the roof is removable, then you can really have some fun.

### WALLPAPER

Regardless of whether the roof is removable or fixed, you'll probably want to add wall coverings of some sort. There are many good reasons for doing this:

- Giving extra strength to fragile walls
- Increasing the quality of reflected light by using light colored wallpaper
- Hiding the wiring used in the lighting
- Adding style and elegance for a more complete creation
- Incorporating personal touches for an intended recipient

Handmade mulberry paper produces a simple, clean finish. The off-white paper is infused with real flower petals and reflects light out the windows better than dark papers. Notice also the green velvet window seat and green felt "carpet" on the floor. These are simple touches that give the room some character.

Every house is different and each has its own challenges. Here are some basic tips, though, that will help you during the process of finishing the interior and "hanging wallpaper" regardless of the house shape or size.

- When applying the wallpaper don't worry about a perfect match with the edges of the window and door openings because the frame that you apply around these openings after the wallpaper is down should cover up any gaps that may occur. Just get as close as you can to the outline of the door and window and if needed, make larger frames!

- Think of the space in terms of blocks and try to tackle those that are most difficult to reach first. I usually do around the doors and windows first and then layer on the big open wall sections last so that their edges overlap the other pieces previously applied.

- When using mulberry or rice papers for your wall covering try to tear the edges rather than cut them with scissors if possible. The torn edges will blend better with the layers below when they are soft and ragged.

- Oftentimes it works best to bring all the vertical pieces beyond the edge of the outside wall (either the top edge or the floor edge, depending on your design) and trim them all off together once the glue has dried using a sharp knife or a pair of sharp scissors.

Green paper frames the door and windows after the wallpaper has been applied. Use a thick, heavy paper for best results. Decorate the frames (if desired) *before* you install.

If your faerie house has a fixed roof, then all of the ends of the wallpaper should extend to the bottom of the house where the floor will be once it is installed. At this point, just double check to make sure that everything is well glued down and then once the glue is dry, trim off the excess with a sharp knife. Test to make sure the house sits level.

After you have covered the walls, you can apply your interior door and window frames and any additional decorations you may wish to add.

Peeking inside. When installed, the roof rests on the twig spokes. Here I have used the same mulberry wallpaper and have added decorative touches to make the interior a little more interesting. These decorations also hide the lighting that circles around the top of the house. In this image you can also see the nicely framed window. The beaded garland, green felt leaves, and vines bring a subtle color scheme into the interior of the house that complements the color scheme on the exterior.

## fINISHING THE TOP EDGE Of THE HOUSE

If your faerie house has a removable roof, you'll need to finish the top edge nicely. Adapt the example below for your house.

### FINISHING WITH A FELT STRIP

If you have any indentations or recesses in your walls, cover those first, then finish the larger lengths of wall after. For this house, I simply cut a strip of brown felt to ⅜ inch and glued it to the raw edge a few inches at a time using wood-colored epoxy, because the clear epoxy has a tendency to bleed into the felt and make it shiny. Hot glue is not durable enough.

TOP: A flat-walled house ready for edge finishing. Walls are uniformly thick and well finished inside and out.

BOTTOM: The finished edge. The felt performs an additional function: it acts as a light barrier to improve the seal of the roof when it is put in place.

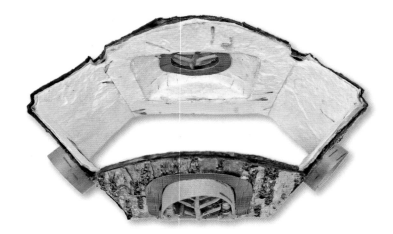

## CREATING A "SHELF" FOR A REMOVABLE ROOF TO REST UPON

On some houses the removable roof rests on eaves that are attached to the house. The Sunflower House is one such example. Because the top side of the eaves is visible when the roof is removed, you may want to finish this large "brim" nicely as well. Page 122 shows the steps for decorating the top side of the eaves for a sunflower-themed house.

As every faerie house is a unique creation, each house with a removable roof may require special, creative solutions for finishing the edges.

Apply a wide strip of felt by folding over the edges on both inside and outside. This adds extra strength to a thinner wall.

## FINISHING A TOP EDGE

If your faerie house has a special theme, adding some creative embellishments can help carry it further. For the house shown below, the flat surface of the eaves (where the roof sits when it is in place) provided another opportunity to celebrate a passion for sunflowers. The application of the silk petals and leaves also helped camouflage the seams in the birch bark, which were already hidden by the twig beams when viewed from below. Plus, the added detail was a nice surprise for the curious viewer.

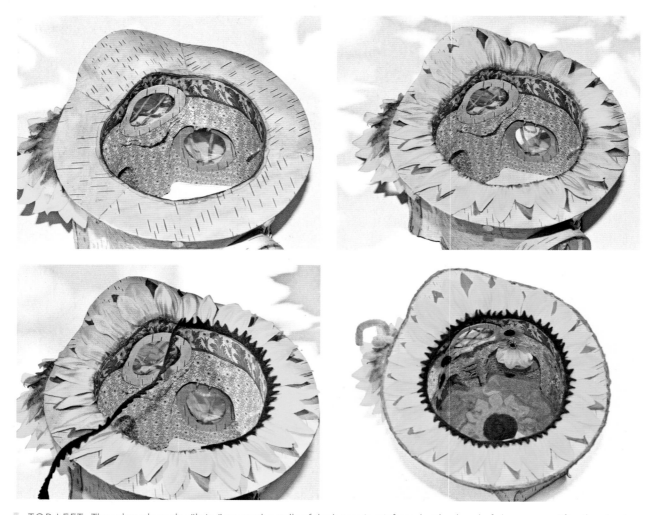

TOP LEFT: The edge where the "brim" meets the walls of the house is reinforced with a bead of clear epoxy. After the glue is dry, you may apply silk botanicals to finish it off.

TOP RIGHT: Apply the green leaves first, then the yellow petals. Using the thinnest dab of clear epoxy on the edge of each petal, glue only at the inner edge.

BOTTOM LEFT: Once the glue is fully dry, apply a trimmed piece of brown felt using hot glue. The strip is wide enough to hide all the shiny epoxy.

BOTTOM RIGHT: For a final touch, carefully glue a fat novelty yarn to the edge of the rim using wood-colored epoxy. This adds protection, durability, and a bit of color to the delicate edge.

## fLOORS

Floors are an important element in faerie house construction because they add strength and stability to the entire piece. Houses with removable roofs make floor installation and decoration a much easier process. Additionally, if the roof does come off and reveals the interior of your faerie house, you may want to maximize your decorating options and fill every inch of the house with crafty bits, including the floor. A creative treatment of the floor can go a long way to creating a stunning interior space.

Structurally speaking, floors made out of acid-free foam-core board work well, or, if you need extra strength and rigidity, you can use specialty plywood made specifically for model and dollhouse building.

There are two basic options for flooring:

- A carefully cut piece that fits perfectly *inside* the walls of the house, OR
- A panel that extends beyond the house to become a base.

There are no hard and fast rules to observe when making floors, though it is helpful to know the difference between these two design options so you can choose the one that will be best for your project.

Floors that go inside the walls:

- Add strength and help maintain the shape and structure of a delicate house.
- Can be installed in such a way that there is a space underneath the floor, which is a handy place to hide battery packs for lighting.
- Are a good design choice for a house that will be attached to or sit on top of an additional decorative base.

Floors that extend beyond the edge of the walls:

- Are a great option for houses that have stiff walls or have rough interiors that are unlikely to be finished.
- Can be extended a little or a lot depending on the design for the base. Sometimes the floor need only extend a half an inch or so beyond the edge of the walls. In some cases it can extend a great deal more than that because it is the entire decorative base.
- Simplify your design because installing the floor also finishes the base of the house nicely.

To make a floor that fits inside the house, trace carefully around the house, then cut out the material on the inside of the line.

Because a house can change its shape and dimensions during the construction process, make the floor pattern after the walls of the house are complete.

This floor and base are one. I cut a piece of dollhouse-grade plywood ½" larger than the house footprint all the way around. I covered the top of the plywood with sage green felt and used epoxy to firmly glue it down. I applied wood-colored epoxy to the very bottom edge of all six walls and centered the house on the felt-covered plywood. Fluffy novelty yarn covers up the raw edge of the house nicely and—as an added bonus—looks a bit like grass. Matching yarn used on the roof visually ties the two elements together.

A welcoming threshold of leaf "steps."

## MAKING A FLOOR

With a removable-roof house you can expand your decorations to include a needle-felted rug or wall-to-wall carpet if space allows. Adding botanicals or sparkly bits makes the rug even more magical.

Once your house is gorgeous inside and out, it's time to cap it all off with a roof and landscape around it so that it comes alive.

TOP LEFT: Applying felt trim to the walls that matches the spiral floor (in background), which will be added next.

TOP RIGHT: A sunny, needle-felted rug for the Sunflower House.

BOTTOM LEFT: Sweet dreamy rug blends perfectly with the walls.

TOP RIGHT: Autumn winds appear to swirl into the house through the front door. This effect is accomplished with needle-felted hand-dyed wool that has paper leaves stitched in place

CHAPTER 5

# finishing touches

## ROOFS, BASES, AND EXTERIOR DETAILS

W ith the basic components of the faerie house built and the interior assembled, it's time to put it all together by finishing the exterior of the house. Roofs offer plenty of opportunity for creativity, as do landscaped bases. Learn the basics and let your creativity do the rest.

### ROOFS

A well-designed and well-crafted roof brings considerable style and visual impact to your faerie house. Even if your house will never go outside, because the roof is what shelters the house from the "elements," having one that looks solid and substantial, yet whimsical, is ideal for tying the faerie house together and making it come together as a visual success.

Design options are infinite. From felted or pinecone roofs to straw roofs that look like thatching, you are limited in your creation only by your imagination. Usually, the roof will extend out over the edge of the house in all directions, and the steeper the angle or pitch, the greater the charm. Roofs can have small porthole windows, gables, or towers that are part of the structure, so it is helpful to have a sketch of what you want before you build.

As noted in the lighting section, there are two main kinds of roofs: those that are attached permanently to the house (fixed roofs) and those that are designed to be removable. A removable roof will need

> The roof and the base should complement each other and the house they surround. If the house is to be a gift, then adding a personal, secret touch will make it even more enchanting.

127

a means of support when it is on the house. Some rest directly on the walls of the house, while others can sit on pegs or faux eaves that are fixed to the house walls. Small tower roofs can be made with a lip that fits inside the walls of the tower.

No matter how the roofs are supported, most have the same basic components.

## THREE MAIN COMPONENTS OF ROOFS

**Base layer.**
On twig frame roofs, this is made of twigs or branches that may or may not be visible from the inside. Some base layers are simply made from heavy paper or stiff felt.

**Middle layer.**
This joins the branches together on a frame roof and gives shape and a degree of sturdiness. On paper roofs, a strengthening layer is applied to the paper.

**Exterior roof covering.**
The top, decorated, outer layer of the roof—what is visible from the outside.

## TYPES OF ROOF COVERINGS

There are many materials that make excellent roof coverings. Let's take a look at some different examples for inspiration.

**Bark roofs.**
You can take pieces of bark apart and use them as shingles or cut and glue together larger sheets to make whimsical roofs. Never remove bark from a living tree.

**Silk botanical roofs.**

These roofs have it all: color, texture, whimsy, and durability. They are a good choice for removable roofs because they are lightweight.

**Live collected flower roofs.**

These are for ephemeral, field-based creations only. Though they only last a very short time, flower roofs are truly magical. You can use them with prebuilt houses for photo shoots in order to preserve the memories forever.

**Live collected leaf roofs.**

Much like flowers, these creations are ephemeral, but beautiful. With some houses, you can get a great photo with live leaves and flowers, and then, if you want to keep the house indoors for longer, you can make a silk botanical facsimile.

**Moss roofs.**

Moss is not the longest-lasting material for a roof covering, but it does make a perfect finish for many woodland faerie houses. Use dried, preserved moss from floral supply stores for indoor houses.

**Pinecone scale roofs.**

Carefully take apart pinecones and use the scales just like you'd use tiny roof shingles.

## Mushrooms/fungi.

If you're planning to keep your faerie house for a long time, the fungi you use must be dried and hard. Some last longer than others.

## Needle felted roof.

All the whimsy you want in a roof! A middle layer of felt is covered with novelty yarns, raw dyed wool, silk and velvet leaves/flowers, beaded vines, or whatever your imagination inspires.

## Single fungus roof.

For houses using a single fungus for the roof, make sure that you choose a variety that is completely dried out and will not fall apart quickly. The fungus should be hard and dense, like soft wood. Many types of shelf fungus will work well. If you live in a humid climate, you may want to seal the fungus with polyurethane. This will reduce the "natural" look, but will keep secondary mold from developing.

# HOW TO MAKE A
# TWIG fRAME ROOf

It may not look very glamorous, but this roof is the goal for this tutorial (for now). This framed roof with a raffia and felt middle layer is an excellent design to learn because it can be adapted for nearly every situation and finishing material. You can also adapt the construction—as I will also describe in this tutorial—to make a removable roof for nearly any cottage. Later I'll show you one way to beautifully finish this roof base.

Read through all of the instructions before you begin so you are clear about what you'll be doing. Most roofs are started once the body of a house has been built, so this tutorial starts at that point.

## MATERIALS fOR BOTH fIXED AND REMOVABLE STYLES

Acid-free cardboard or matboard

Thicker twigs for roof beams

Matched, slightly curved twigs for rafters

Long twig for central support pole

Raffia

Felt (brown and green used here)

Wood-colored epoxy glue

Small piece of waxed paper (3 x 3")
for removable roof

Hot glue sticks

## TOOLS

Pencil

Scissors

X-Acto knife

Hand pruners

Wire snips

Needle-pointed pruning shears

Sandpaper

Fine-toothed flat saw

Hot glue gun

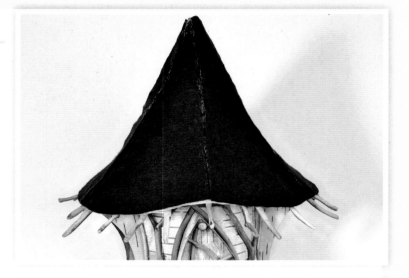

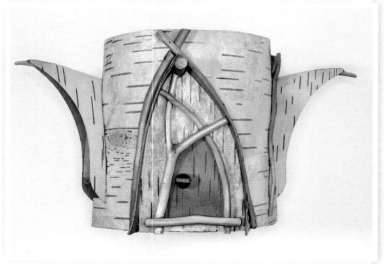

BOTH: Examples of a finished twig frame roof and the accompanying house.

# MAKING THE ROOF

## STEP 1

**For both roof styles:** Turn the house upside down onto a sheet of acid-free cardboard or matboard. Trace around the outside circumference of the house with a pencil. Cut out the cardboard/matboard slightly *inside* your pencil line so that the piece of cardboard will fit snugly inside the top of the house and function as a ceiling.

**For the removable roof:** Insert the circle into the top of the house and *lightly* tack in place with three to four small drops of hot glue—it will be removed later.

## STEP 2

**For both roof styles:** Cut six or more roof beams using the fine-toothed saw for flat ends. The number of beams is a style choice. Eight is a good average. The beams should all be approximately the same diameter and length and nicely finished on the ends.

**For the fixed roof:** Glue cardboard circle in place so that the cardboard is lower than the top edge of the house wall by the thickness of the beams.

**For the removable roof:** Do not do this step.

## STEP 3

**For the fixed roof:** Use the X-Acto knife to cut U-shaped notches in the top edge of the house wall to hold the roof beams. Attach the roof beams to the body of the house using epoxy glue on the inside of the notches, extending the beams inside the house a little bit. Do this one beam at a time, letting the glue set before you move to the next one. That way you can make sure all of the beams stay level.

**For the removable roof:** Do not do this step.

(Handy trick: Once the glue begins to set, turn the house upside down onto a flat surface and adjust the beam so it is pressed flat while the glue finishes setting. Do this with each beam and all the beams will be flat and true.)

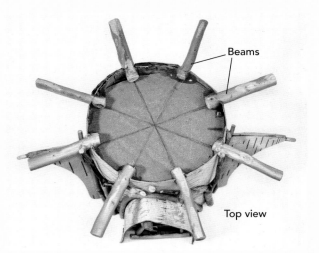

Beams

Top view

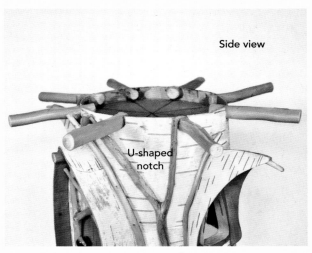

Side view

U-shaped notch

**For the fixed roof:** Here is a view of how the house looks with all the beams in position for a fixed roof but before they are glued permanently in place. Note how the beams extend slightly to the inside of the house. This allows for extra surface area for the glue to make a solid contact and creates strong joints to support the rest of the roof.

## STEP 4

**For both roof styles:** Create and affix the eaves ring that will support the rafters. To determine the shape and dimensions of the ring, turn the house upside down onto a clean sheet of matboard and trace around the walls of the house.

**For the fixed roof:** On the paper mark the location of outer ends of the beams. Remove the house. Draw a circle ½ to ¾ inch inside those beam ends. Also draw a circle ½ inch *inside* the outline of the house wall. Cut out the ring.

**For the removable roof:** Trace around the house wall first. Lay down a few roof beams and trace another circle that is ½ to ¾ inch inside those beam ends. Remove house and retrace the inner line ⅛ inch inside. Cut out the circle.

**For both roof styles:** Collect twigs that will be used for the roof rafters. You will also need a piece of acid-free matboard to create the eaves ring. You will need one good twig rafter for each roof beam, plus some additional twigs that are similar in size and appearance. The main rafter twigs should all have a similar diameter and shape. If you want a pleasing bell-shaped roof, select rafter twigs that have a slight curve at one end and are straight at the other.

**For the fixed roof:** This is how the cardboard cutout should fit the house while it is stilling on top of the beams. Note that the front of the house is indicated with an arrow drawn in pencil on the top of the eaves ring. This helps to ensure that the correct side is down—not all structures are perfectly symmetrical.

## STEP 5

**For both roof styles:** Cover the matboard eaves ring with your choice of desired material, such as felt or paper to give a decorative finish to the underside of the eaves. Cut the decorative material so that it is larger around the outside edge and smaller than the inside edge of the ring. Fold over the outside edge and glue the fabric to the board well, so that the good side faces down.

**For the fixed roof:** When you have completely covered the ring, glue it (good side facing down) to the beams using wood-colored epoxy.

**For the removable roof:** Once the ring is covered, place it on the table good side up. Attach it to the house by applying a bead of hot glue to the rim of the house wall, then quickly turning the house upside down and centering it onto the felted ring. Take the twig beams and glue them evenly around the ring with wood-colored epoxy. Apply glue also to the end of each beam where it is meeting up with the wall of the house. Do this step well because the weight of the roof will rest on this ring.

## STEP 6

**For both roofs:** The height of this support pole will define the total height of the roof. To determine the ideal height for this central pole, hold one of the selected rafter twigs in position from the top of the support pole out past one of the twig beams to make sure that enough of the curved end of the rafter twig extends well beyond the outer end of the roof beams. The height of the roof is simply a matter of personal preference and not a specified measurement, so make this adjustment to your own taste. Just make sure that your rafters are long enough to extend beyond the roof beams when the other end is attached at the peak/top of the main pole support. You will need to lower the height of the support pole if the roof rafters do not meet the beams properly.

**For the fixed roof:** Glue the long straight support pole twig to the center of your cardboard insert using epoxy glue.

**For the removable roof:** Do the same thing, only glue very lightly—you will remove this later.

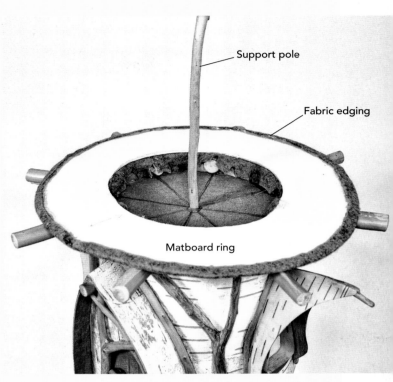

Support pole

Fabric edging

Matboard ring

The felt-covered eaves ring glued onto the beams for the fixed-roof design. The central twig is also glued firmly in place. For removable roofs, the ends of the twigs inside the ring do not show as they butt up against the wall of the house. Also, the central support twig is very lightly glued in place to be removed later.

## STEP 7A: PRIMARY RAFTERS

**For both roofs:** You will now begin to install the individual rafter twigs. Do this step carefully because the shape of your roof depends on good technique and attention to detail in this step. Use the straight ends of the rafter twigs at the peak of the roof and the curved ends at the bottom (beam end) to give a pleasing silhouette to your roof. Cut the specially selected matching rafter twigs to approximately the same length and trim the curved ends so they all have approximately the same angle cut to the others.

**For the fixed roof:** Use wood-colored epoxy, not hot glue, to glue the rafters in place. Watch for drips and remove them before they set. Use wood-colored epoxy glue to attach each primary rafter to the central support pole and to one side of the appropriate roof beam. Use small amounts of epoxy glue to simply anchor the rafters in place. Once they are all dry, you can apply more epoxy to each rafter joint to make sure it is solid, taking care not to drip.

**For the removable roof:** Wrap the top of the center pole in the waxed paper to keep glue from sticking to it. Secure with tape. Use tiny drops of hot glue to affix each rafter to each beam. Be careful to not get glue on the felt/eaves ring. Use epoxy glue to affix the other ends of the rafters to each other as they rest on the waxed paper covering the tip of the central support pole. You're going to need to remove the roof afterward, at which time you will reinforce all the joints. Glue just enough to hold it together.

## STEP 7B: SECONDARY RAFTERS

**For both roofs:** Once the primary rafters are securely attached it is time to apply the secondary rafters. These are the next-best twigs in your collection and ideally should have curved ends similar to the primary rafters. Trim off ½ inch from the top end of the twig. Glue the secondary rafters in place so that the curved end is attached to one of the beams already attached to a primary rafter and the straight end is attached to the adjoining primary rafter. Attach all secondary rafters in the same manner.

**For the removable roof:** Do the same thing, using small dabs of epoxy at the roof top and tiny drops of hot glue to (temporarily) attach to the beams.

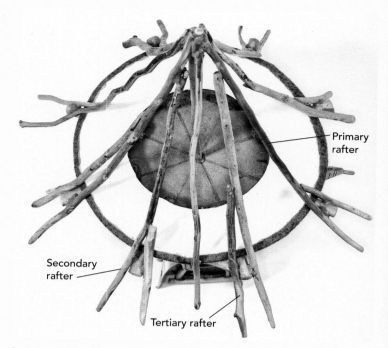

Primary rafter

Secondary rafter

Tertiary rafter

Select the four best rafter twigs that match one another and use these as your primary rafters to be installed first. They should be equally spaced, roughly speaking, one at each quadrant, and are attached first to help establish the roof shape. Trim the top ends of the primary rafter twigs so that there is a good surface joining the central pole, then add the rest of the rafters.

## STEP 7C: TERTIARY RAFTERS

**For both roofs:** After the primary and secondary rafters are attached, it is time to install the tertiary rafters. These twigs should be about one-third the length of the secondary rafters. Attach these twigs onto the opposite side of each beam where the primary or secondary rafter is already attached. Glue these into position so that the outside ends roughly match the primary and secondary rafter ends to make a full and complete circle around the edge of the roof. Each beam should now have two rafters attached to it.

**For the fixed roof:** Use epoxy glue at both ends.

**For the removable roof:** Use epoxy glue at the top and tiny drops of hot glue at the beam/bottom ends.

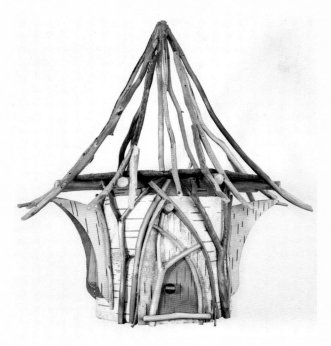

## STEP 7D: DOORWAY RAFTER

**For both roofs:** The final rafter to be put in place will be a single rafter that is centered over the doorway. This rafter can be longer or shorter than the primary or secondary rafters, it is simply a matter of personal preference. Note that a support beam from below is not required for this rafter. Just make sure that it follows the same general shape and curve of the primary and secondary rafters.

**For the fixed roof:** Glue with epoxy at both ends, but attach to the eaves ring if there is no available beam for this rafter.

**For the removable roof:** Attach with epoxy glue at the top end only. Allow the lower end to be free for now. For this roof only, go back to all the epoxy joints above the ring line and reinforce with extra epoxy. Glue the tops of the rafters to one another, not to the central pole.

Roof with all rafters glued into place. Both styles of roofs should look similar to this.

From below, both styles of houses should look similar to this except the removable roof will have tiny dots of hot glue joining the rafters to the beams. This image shows how the tertiary rafters are matched to the primary and secondary rafters on either side of each beam. You can see how important it is not to let epoxy glue drip while you are attaching rafters for a fixed roof. The key is patience! Let each piece dry before gluing the next.

## STEP 8A

**For both roofs:** Using a hot glue gun, attach strands of raffia to the rafters in a spiral pattern starting from the top of the roof and working downward. Only a small drop of hot glue is necessary to attach the raffia to each rafter. Space the strands approximately ½ inch apart at the top of the roof and space them gradually closer together as you approach the bottom. Apply the raffia below the eaves ring but not all the way to the ends of the rafters. Space these last few strands closer together.

## STEP 8B

**For the removable roof:** Using a sharp craft knife, cut the twig rafter frame free from the beams at the glue dots. Gently remove the twig frame. Pull out the central support pole and discard. Pull out the initial cardboard insert circle and discard. Pull out any loose bits of waxed paper and discard. Clean and trim any glue drips. Apply small dabs of epoxy glue to all wood joints if needed. Replace roof onto house.

## STEP 8C

**For both roofs:** If you plan to apply lighting to your roof, do that next before applying the felt layer.

**For the removable roof:** Keep in mind that the lights applied to the roof will not be able to be attached to the body of the house. However, a lighted roof can illuminate the interior of a single room house very well.

## STEP 9

**For both roofs:** Install the underlayer for the roof skin. Ordinary felt works really well for this step because it can be stretched slightly if needed to fit the natural curves and bumps made by the twig rafters while still giving a smooth continuous cover upon which the finished roof materials will be applied. The color of felt to be used depends on the material you will be using on the outer, visible layer of the roof. Silk botanical or needle felted roofs work better with green felt as the underlayer because it gives a natural look.

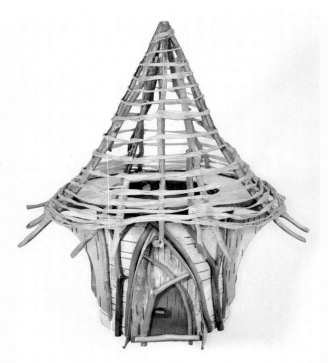

Strands of raffia are wrapped around the roof support structure to strengthen it and provide a gluing surface for the roof covering.

Triangular strips of felt are glued to the roof structure to create the roof underlayer.

**For both roofs (continued):** Begin by cutting out triangular-shaped pieces of felt that closely match the space between the major rafters. Depending on the size and shape of your roof this can usually be achieved using six large pieces. The important issue is to match up the edges of the felt with primary and secondary rafters going all the way from top of the roof to the bottom of the raffia. Apply the felt with hot glue. Many small drops of glue are preferable to large amounts that might drip down onto the inside of the house. Start at the top of the triangle and work down. If desired you can also attach the felt to the freely floating raffia if desired, but the felt needs to be firmly attached to all the wood raters.

**For the fixed roof:** Turn the house over and trim off the excess felt at the bottom edge, leaving a ⅛-inch margin of felt that extends beyond the last raffia strand.

**For the removable roof:** Simply remove the roof to trim the felt.

Stretch and adjust the felt triangle during the attachment process as needed for a smooth fit, but do so gently with the removable roof as it is more delicate.

Here we have the finished framing and roof ready to be decorated with the final layer of covering materials.

## COVERING THE FRAMED ROOF WITH PINECONE SCALES AND SILK BOTANICALS

Now we can apply a decorative finish to the roof. The steps are the same for both the fixed and removable roofs.

### YOU WILL NEED:

Pinecone scales

Silk botanicals

Acorn cap

Goldenrod burl, or other suitable finial seedpod or pinecone

Florist's wire

Sandpaper

Needle-nose pruners

Drill

Here are the various silk leaves for this roofing project. You can see a variety of sizes, colors, and textures, but they all look good together.

## STEP I

Prepare the pinecone scales. Any large conifer cone can be used. These cones are from sugar pines, which I purchased from reputable sellers on eBay who collect them in a sustainable way.

Cut off the individual scales as close to the core as possible. With some cones you can pull the scales off the core with just your fingers. This is the preferred method because it causes the least amount of damage to the scales. Discard split/broken scales.

Trim the scales to make them ready for use. Most scales have a tough ligament where it was connected to the cone. Trim that off. You may also need to reshape the lower edge of some scales with sandpaper so they are more uniform and rounded.

The image [above] shows this process. Scale #1 shows the top and bottom views of the scale as it came off the cone. Scale #2 shows how the top of the scale has been trimmed and rounded using the needle nose pruners and sandpaper. Scale #3 shows how the bottom edge has been trimmed and rounded using only sandpaper. This scale is now ready to be applied in a roofing project.

Most methods of applying the final finishing layer of the roof begin at the bottom of the roof and work up to the top. Another general rule of thumb to keep in mind is that larger objects or items are usually placed near the bottom and the smaller ones near the top. This makes the roof look balanced and also provides the most efficient coverage with whatever material you are using for decorating your roof.

takes longer to apply. Whichever glue you choose to use, application is fairly straightforward: simply dab on a suitable amount of glue to just the top of the back of the scale and press the scale down into position close to the previous scale. You may need to trim and adjust the scales for a tighter side-by-side fit (before you apply the glue) as you go along.

Once the first row of scales is glued on, add a few tendrils of preserved Spanish moss, using the hot glue gun. After applying the layer of moss, add the second row of scales like fish scales: apply a single scale over the space between the two scales that are on the row below. This gives a lovely decorative pattern. Trim the width of scales as needed.

The roof now has two complete rows of scales applied so you can see how the overlapping pattern works. You could cover the whole roof this way. Usually the last few layers require careful trimming and fitting of the scales so that they are perfectly matched and sit side by side with no gaps. Finish the roof using the epoxy glue instead of hot glue for the last three rows, if you chose this method.

Another option is to apply something completely different yet harmonious. This could be done with pine bark pieces, a different species of pinecone scale—or you could use silk botanicals, which is what we will add next.

## STEP 2

Apply the scales as shingles. Use the largest prepared scales at the bottom, gradually using smaller and smaller scales as you work up the roof. Begin laying down the lowest/first row of scales starting at the back of the house, working around the roof returning to the starting point. The reason: sometimes the final few scales need to be trimmed or narrowed in order to finish the row. Keep that less visible by starting in the back. Always use the best materials on the front.

Hot glue is easiest for this step, but tends to come away from the scales over time. Epoxy is better but

Notice how the first row of scales extends well beyond the edge of felt but not as far as the edge of the rafter twigs.

Work upward from the roof eave, starting with your longest pinecone scales. Layer in Spanish moss strands as you go.

## STEP 3

Apply the silk botanicals. Just as with the scales you'll want to have all of your botanicals sorted according to size, color, etc., before you actually begin.

Begin at the back of the house using the largest leaves first. You don't need to apply glue to the entire leaf surface—in fact it's best not to. Rather, apply the glue to just the top third of the leaf back and let the rest of the leaf float freely after it is stuck onto the roof. Optional: Continue to apply small tendrils of the Spanish moss along with the leaves to help visually tie the two layers together.

Alternate the colors and textures of the leaves while applying for a more natural-looking and interesting roof. Continue working in this manner using smaller and smaller leaves going up the roof until you reach the very top.

Use smaller silk botanicals as you move higher up on the roof. Save the smallest leaves for the peak, adding small tendrils of Spanish moss in the layers as you go.

## STEP 4

Finish the roof with a decorative finial. You can build your finial on a tiny funnel to help control the shape. The curls of birch bark used for this finial add another layer of texture that also harmonizes with the walls of the house. Glue the finial together using the wood-colored epoxy, so it will be sturdy even though it looks delicate.

Insert a short, sturdy wire into the top of the point of the roof and glue it in place with epoxy glue (you may need to drill a hole in your rafters for a secure fit). Once the wire is secure, lower the finial (without the acorn cap) onto the wire and fill the space with generous amounts of epoxy resin for an absolutely secure junction. Watch out for drips! Drill a small hole in the acorn cap and lower it onto the wire, glue in place. Finally, drill the goldenrod burl to accept the wire and glue it into place.

Optional: Use extra-fine sandpaper to finish the ends of the rafters in whatever way appeals to you.

Congratulations on building a great roof for your house!

Create a finial and attach it to the peak with wire. If you do not have these exact materials, improvise! Other finial options include a small pinecone, a walnut, a large acorn, an unusual piece of driftwood, or a shell. Use what nature provides.

For removable roofs, you may wish to add some sort of liner to your roof. Here paper "petals" have been glued in place inside this twig-framed roof.

# HOW TO CREATE A
# NO-FRAME REMOVABLE ROOF WITH SILK BOTANICALS

In this lesson you will learn how to build a no-frame roof, which makes a great base for simple removable roofs. You can use heavy paper, birch bark, felt, or any other thin, flexible material for this base. Adapt the technique for different materials and for polygonal houses.

You will also learn how to apply silk botanicals, which add lots of color without adding lots of weight to your faerie house roof. Additionally, you can have *so much* fun mixing up different elements and textures for a colorful, organic look. Any sort of silk flower, leaf, or fern can be used, just apply them using the same basic technique.

### MATERIALS FOR ROOF FOUNDATION

Watercolor (or other heavy, acid-free) paper

White glue mixed with water

Green tissue paper

Sheet of waxed paper larger than the top of the house

Hot glue sticks

### MATERIALS FOR DECORATIVE COVER

Silk flower petals in varying sizes (take apart large silk flowers or purchase loose petals)

Silk leaves

Decorative paper for lining (optional)

Hot glue sticks

Epoxy glue

### TOOLS

Scissors

Tweezers

Glue gun

Brush to apply white glue mix

## MAKING THE NO-FRAME
## ROOF FOUNDATION

### STEP 1

To begin, make a basic cone that fits the circle of the body
of the house. Heavy watercolor paper works well, and it
can be found at good art supply stores. Use hot glue or
epoxy to glue the paper together. This is one of the few
times when I like to use hot glue because it's fast-drying
and relatively strong. To make the "brim" for the roof, cut
out two arcs of paper as shown. Each house will be different
so adapt your pattern accordingly.

### STEP 2

Approximate the angle of the brim to the cone by taping
it together. Once you're satisfied with the shape, glue it
in place.

### STEP 3

Once the paper foundation is satisfactory, give it a little
strength using tissue paper and glue. I like to use green
tissue paper or thin, gauzy fabric to give the no-frame roof
strength and a consistent color. Tear strips of tissue paper
into small strips. Use a brush to coat the strips with slightly
thinned white glue. Apply the pieces to the roof overlapping
the strips as you go. Use the glue mixture sparingly—just
enough to anchor the pieces in place. If you use too much
glue-mix you run the risk of making the base too soggy
and it could bubble and warp. Cover the no-frame roof
completely on the top side. Let it dry. Add an extra layer of
tissue paper to the edge of the brim for added strength. Let
dry again. Turn the roof over and repeat the process on the
interior. If you plan to line the roof with decorative paper,
you do not need to cover the inside of the cone.

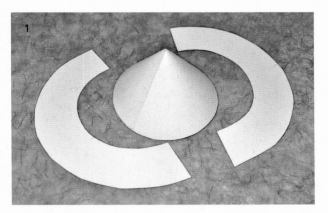

## STEP 4

When the roof has dried to a leathery feel, put a piece of waxed paper over the rim of the house, and put the roof on the faerie house to make sure everything is fitting properly. Gently press and mold to fit well.

## STEP 5

Check the roof from all angles to make sure that it is fitting as snuggly as possible against the base of the faerie house. Let dry overnight. Remove and discard wax paper.

The paper roof may seem small at first, but once the botanicals start getting layered onto it, the roof will become much larger in appearance. The ends of the petals or leaves look best if they extend well beyond the edges of the paper base, for a fluffy, natural look.

# DECORATING WITH SILK BOTANICALS

## STEP I

Because the inside of the roof is going to be visible when you remove it from the house, give it a nice finish. Turn the roof over. Apply some yellow petals to the underside of the brim. Use hot glue sparingly; you don't want to add too much weight to the roof. Because these petals will barely show, it's okay if they're not of the best quality. Next, apply the green silk leaves, making sure that they overlap one another so that no paper brim is visible. Make sure to extend the edges of the leaves up inside the cone, past the brim. Cover the brim completely. Turn the roof over for the next step.

Many silk leaves and ferns come with an added rib that mimics the veins of the leaf. Leave this attached if it gives added shape and support where you need some. Otherwise, you can pull off the rib.

## STEP 2

You should see the petal ends and the leaves from the underside of the roof extend past the edge of the brim. Check around the entire edge of the brim to make sure all of the petals and leaves from the underside are securely anchored to the edge of the brim.

Begin adding the first layer of silk botanicals to the top side of the paper roof, placing one petal tip in the space between the two petals from the underside.

Use two-part epoxy (mix equal amounts in small batches) or hot glue, but use sparingly. The epoxy is stronger, but test it first on scrap pieces because it sometimes leaks through the silk fabric and gives an undesired result. The wood-colored epoxy seems to soak in less.

Apply the first layer of petals so that none of the paper roof shows underneath or between the petals. Apply the glue to the upper fourth (top) end of the petals only and leave the pointy ends free to float for a more natural look.

Always test the glue on your materials first to make sure that you're happy with how the glue interacts with the material.

## STEP 3

After applying the first row of petals, add the next row. Again, place the next petal so that the point rests in the space between the two petals on the layer below. Use the largest pieces for the bottom/first rows, middle-sized pieces for the middle of the roof, and save the tiniest pieces for the top of the roof. If the silk botanicals are all the same size, you can trim them so that you have different sizes. Follow the same steps applying smaller and smaller botanicals as you ascend the roof until you come to the apex.

Try to make the placement of the silk botanicals very slightly irregular on each layer. Mix it up as the layers go up the roof. Layer in a bit of ribbon, or leaves of a different texture/material. Break up any regular patterns that may be forming—it will look more natural if it's slightly random, like it would be in nature.

## STEP 4

If your artificial flower comes with a stem, you may be able to modify it to act as the finial for the roof. In this example, the green petals of the back of the artificial sunflower were applied in the same manner as the large petals to come all the way up to the point of the roof. I bent the artificial stem into a pleasing design.

Attach the stem from the artificial flower onto the apex of the roof. Because this junction point is critical to the integrity of the roof, use epoxy glue to make sure that the stem is glued solidly. Use a wire connector before applying the glue for a stronger bond (see above in the previous roof tutorial). If you're not using an artificial stem, you can simply bring the botanicals up until they make a natural point or use an acorn or seedpod as your finial. Whatever you use, make sure it's glued down really well.

## STEP 5

To finish the inside of the roof, make a cone of decorative paper or fabric and trim to the proper size so that it overlaps any of the raw edges. When you have determined that the cone of decorative material fits nicely, glue it all in place really well with the hot glue. Optional: Add a bit of fun trim around the raw edge of the liner to seal it up well.

The finished roof sitting on the finished house.

In the example to the right, I've used basically the same technique that I used with the sunflower roof but with different materials. This roof is constructed using silk and velvet leaves in autumn colors. If you look closely, you'll see that there are also silk ferns and sprigs of glittery twigs in between the layers. To give the best effect, keep the outer/lower edges of the leaves or petals free from glue. This creates a more natural look.

Feel free to add bits of sparkly material, yarn, ribbons, or whatever you like in the layers as you go up the roof. They will add interest and dazzle to your faerie house.

## BASES & LANDSCAPING

There are so many options for faerie house bases! The base can be a major part of the look and feel of the house. Depending on the design, a base can be added after a house is completed or can even be the initial inspiration for creating a house.

Let's look at some bases to get "grounded" in the possibilities and see some construction details.

TOP: This base forms the foundation for the tree trunk–like structures that support the house and gazebo. The base also provides structure for the waterfall and mossy landscaping.

BOTTOM: A modest base can still be lovely and should harmonize with the house design and materials.

Be certain that the bottom of the house is plumb and level before permanently affixing it to the base, unless you *want* a lopsided look.

TOP LEFT: More elaborate designs can provide additional opportunities for miniature landscaping.

MIDDLE LEFT: A base can help tell a story. Here is an "island" waiting for its house.

BOTTOM LEFT: Here there (may) be dragons in a crystal-lined cave beneath a faerie castle!

TOP RIGHT: Don't forget to decorate the back!

BOTTOM RIGHT: Some bases add considerable height for better viewing. This house can come off the base to be taken to other locations.

A base is cut to fit from dollhouse-grade plywood.

## HOW TO MAKE A SIMPLE BASE

Here is an example of the simplest solution for the bottom of a faerie house. A piece of dollhouse-grade birch plywood has been cut out in an oval-like shape slightly larger than the actual footprint of the house. The finished house is then glued onto the base using wood-colored epoxy glue. A small piece of preserved moss is added at the front entrance, but otherwise the polished plywood is visible as an undecorated yet sturdy base for the house.

You may wish to add several small circles of felt to the very bottom of the base if the house is going to be placed on fine wood furniture. The felt pads help prevent scratches.

Preserved moss is attached to the base to create an entry mat.

TOP LEFT: A more organic version of a modest base. Decorations add great appeal and unify house with base.

TOP RIGHT: A top-heavy house needs extra stability. This tall house is not a good design for a stand-alone structure. To firmly attached it to a broader base, first glue felt to the bottom rim of the finished house with a generous application of epoxy. Next, glue pebbles to the outside wall and the felt for extra strength.

LEFT: The base slab of wood is minimally prepared by trimming and sanding any rough edges on the top and bottom surfaces. The raw side/edge is left as natural as possible. Use liberal amounts of epoxy on both the base and the bottom of the felt and then press the house into place for a secure bond. See the next page for landscape decorations.

LEFT: Finished and decorated base from page 153.

ABOVE: Stone steps and mossy accents help seamlessly blend house with base. The base was created first, and the house was then crafted to fit it very precisely. Applications of small stones add physical weight, which can add helpful stability to a lightweight cottage.

BELOW: This base is made from ⅛" cabinet-grade plywood and has subtle contours built from multiple layers of felt. Preserved moss, silk botanicals, river stones, and faux moss-covered stones are used as landscaping materials. The tiny mushrooms help with a sense of scale and bring in spots of color. The edge of the plywood is covered with a ¼"-wide strip of green felt. Another option is to paint the sanded plywood edge with acrylic paint before it is landscaped.

TOP: A thick piece of natural birch bark has been trimmed and shaped into an asymmetrical base. There is a smaller circle of ⅛" plywood underneath the bark, but it is invisible from the top. It was added to give extra support to the base and also to keep the bark from curling. The main house is attached to the birch bark using liberal applications of wood-colored epoxy glue. Several types of silk botanicals are applied around the base for landscaping. Notice how the leaves are glued in place to give a natural appearance.

MIDDLE: When creating a base like this, use several different kinds of silk leaves to maximize the visual impact and create a more natural-looking setting. Adding a few sprigs of climbing greenery to mimic vines on the walls visually ties the house to the base and gives it a sense of age. There is a battery pack hiding in the foliage on the left.

BOTTOM: A good base will add physical and visual stability to your faerie house creation.

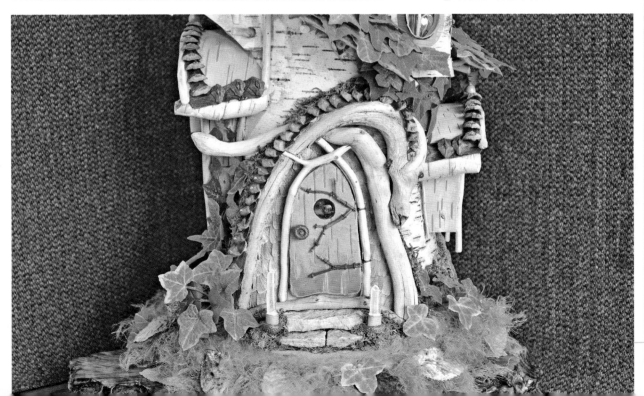

## PATHWAYS TO HOME

The making of paths, steps, and stairs is a deeply intuitive part of the whole faerie house process. I've learned this from watching children making faerie houses either alone or in a group. At some point, usually after the main components of the house are complete, kids will almost always lavish great care on the pathway to the house. It is as if some part of our deep, innocent selves knows that finding our way to the place of magic and sanctuary must be mapped.

I like to think of stairs, steps, and paths as the metaphorical bridges our imagination needs to help us connect to the magical world. While the front door allows us to actually enter the magical space within, our eyes instinctively seek our *way* to that door by following paths, stairs, and steps. Everyone will have his or her own style and method for crafting this part of their dream house. Some builders like to create extravagant bridges and bordered paths. For others, a humble set of stepping stones will do.

Here are some constructions to help spark your own creativity.

LEFT: Stone stairs enhance any faerie house entrance.

BELOW: Tiny strips of green felt look like moss when added to stonework for tiny houses. Rough up the cut edges of the felt with sandpaper for a softer edge and tuck in as you glue the stone in place.

To lay in a set of simple stairs, start with uniformly thick stones. Then, beginning at the bottom, rest the front edge of the second stone onto the back edge of the first stone. Repeat until you have the height you want. You may need to provide additional support behind and under some stones.

LEFT: Out in the wild, a meander of sandstone steps brings the viewer up the thyme-covered slopes right to the round front door.

ABOVE: In this example, tiny bracket fungi are being used as a stairway to the front door as well as for additional decorations on the exterior of the house.

## TWIGGY BITS

Making the little twig details for faerie houses is a lot of fun and doesn't require a lot of skill or equipment. What it does require, however, is patience, a delicate touch, and a little bit of creative ingenuity. Here are some samples of twig work to help you get inspired to experiment with embellishing your own projects with these delicate details. All of the components in these images were made with very simple tools: a fine-toothed saw, a sharp knife for trimming and carving, sandpaper for smoothing, and wood-colored epoxy for gluing the twigs together. In some cases raffia or moss were added for decoration.

 The balcony and railing installed.

TOP: This tiny footbridge was made using a similar technique as on page 158. The curved footbridge base was made first. There are three crossbars hidden underneath. Next, the upright posts were cut and carved to fit, and finally the curved railing was attached.

BOTTOM: A balcony with a twig railing and a mossy carpet were designed for a special location. Choose a long twig with interesting curves and details for the railing and similarly colored twigs for posts.

OPPOSITE TOP: A simple footbridge is made from two similarly curved twigs of the same length. They are joined together at regular intervals by crosswise twigs glued underneath the bridge. The joints are wrapped with raffia to conceal the glue. Once all the crossbars are in place and decorated with spiraling strands of raffia, a long narrow strip of birch bark is cut, fitted, and glued in between the two railings. These simple bridges can be flat or arched.

OPPOSITE BOTTOM: This faerie footbridge leads to a magical teahouse set in the middle of a forest stream. It was constructed using the same techniques as the other footbridge. The rustic nature of the sections enhanced the whole setting for this tiny tea house.

**Tip:** In most instances it is better to use the lighter-colored twigs so that they show up against most backgrounds and houses, which are usually darker. Look for light-colored twigs for your delicate railings and other twig work details, such as mullions in windows. That way, your careful and patient craftwork will be shown to its best advantage. Fresh weeping willow is an excellent choice for beginner twig work, because the branches are flexible and easy to work with when they are green and they dry to a lovely golden honey brown. They are also common trees that can be found in many urban and suburban environments and parks all around the world.

TOP LEFT: These tiny structures add a lot of charm and style, but they do take time and patience to make. This little gem, at 3½" tall, took more than eight hours to make! The "vines" are actually covered wires that allowed the miniature gazebo to be lighted.

TOP RIGHT: If the space you want to decorate with railings is too small for twigs, you can try using dried grapevine tendrils instead. They come in strange and crazy shapes, but they add a wonderful sense of wildness for tiny balconies and windows. The tendrils from wild or cultivated grapes need to be collected in the fall after they have dried on the vine. Use needle pruners to snip them off and clear epoxy to glue in place, as the wood-colored epoxy will show against these dark tendrils.

RIGHT: Don't forget to have fun decorating your tiny twig details too. Wrap with ribbons or bring out beads and berries for holiday cheer. A birch bark bucket of berries and a tiny wreath completes the festive look.

It is my sincere hope that the images and instructions in these pages have filled you with inspiration and courage to try your own hand at making something magical from nature's bounty. Whether you are just a beginner or an experienced crafter, these pages should give you the information you need to get started on a whole new adventure imagining new dimensions of creative expression and joy.

Please remember to collect your own materials from nature with respect and gratitude but always do so in a sustainable fashion. Be kind to Nature and she will be kind to you.

Now it's time to put everything together and build a couple of delightful houses from the ground up!

Fireflies and a faerie house—a midsummer's dream.

# CHAPTER 6

# Building a Faerie House from the Ground, up

The Green Dreams House in a garden setting.

This chapter is going to be a bit different. Here you will find step-by-step instructions on how to construct two different faerie houses. I specifically designed these two houses for this book and photographed them step-by-step as I built them. The first house, the Green Dreams House, will show you many of the basic techniques needed to help you get started to successfully build a faerie house. There will be written instructions and copious photos to guide you along. This house features curved-wall construction with basic door, window, and fixed-frame roof components, all finished off with an integrated flat base.

The second tutorial is advanced and has less text describing the process. This tutorial follows the creation of the Golden Cottage, with flat walls with an arched, hinged door, complex mullioned windows, a bay window feature, and an elaborate removable, lighted roof. The house also features a sculpted and landscaped base. These two houses together were specifically designed to teach you all the key techniques you will need to then set off down your own path of creativity of making charming and unique faerie houses.

As I have suggested many times already in these pages, please read all the instructions and be very familiar with the process before starting. Work slowly and carefully and use lots of patience during each phase of construction, and you will be rewarded with a sweet little house that you can be proud of!

# GREEN DREAMS HOUSE

The main body for this house is made from a tube of birch bark that I found in the forest. As with all of the wild-collected materials, it is necessary to clean, dry, and prepare found pieces for use. If you do not have access to birch bark in your area, it is possible to purchase flat sheets and tubes from various suppliers on the Internet—especially on eBay. Feel free to adapt any of the materials in these tutorials to ones that are plentiful in your region. For this project, the tube of birch bark is approximately 6 inches in diameter and 8 inches tall, but this house can be made at any scale as long as you keep things relatively proportional.

## ▮1▮ MAKE AND INSTALL THE DOOR

Follow the instructions in Chapter 3 on page 60 to make the twig-framed door in vestibule. Once you have made the door, trim and adjust the back edge of the vestibule so that it fits snugly against the curved wall of the main house. Once that adjustment has been made, glue the vestibule to the house using wood-colored epoxy glue. After the epoxy has set, apply a decorative twig to either edge of the junction where the vestibule meets the house—again using wood-colored epoxy. ***Note:*** *Unless otherwise specified, you should use epoxy for most of these constructions.*

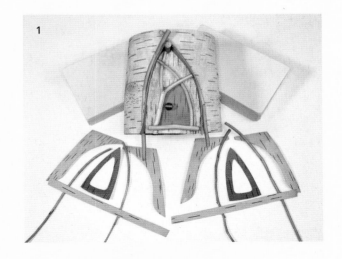

## ▮2▮ MAKE AND INSTALL THE WINDOWS

Next, gather your materials for the two triangular-shaped windows with awnings and install them in the house. The tutorial for these windows is found in Chapter 3 on page 80.

Image 2A is the main body of the house and the installed door with its vestibule, as well as one of the windows with the decorative awning. Note how the twigs have been glued over the junction areas to help strengthen the joints and hide any imperfect bonding.

Notice the way using different colors of birch bark for the awnings and the door can add harmonious subtlety to the main body of the house. In image 2B, the decorative twig outlining the window on the right has been applied.

That hasn't been done to the window on the left. If one wanted to use dark twigs as decorative accents, the resulting look would be different and striking, which may be more appealing to your taste. What is important is to use materials that are durable, beautiful, and pleasing to your eye, so don't feel that you have to replicate exactly what is being shown here.

The apex of the window awnings and the door vestibule are all at approximately the same distance away from the top edge of the house. In this tutorial example that distance is approximately 1 inch on the nearly 8-inch-tall house. You will need a proportional margin for the next step.

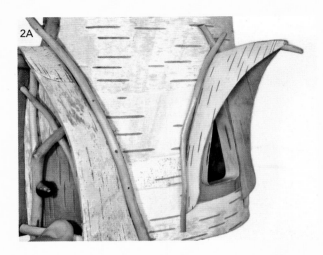

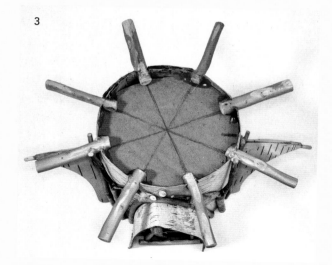

3

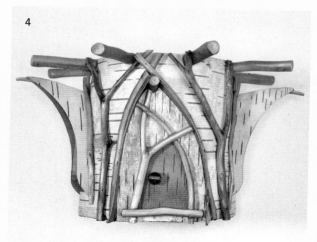

4

### 3 INSTALL ROOF BEAMS

Following the instructions in Chapter 5 on page 132 for the fixed, framed roof tutorial, begin by creating and installing your roof beams as instructed. If your house is smaller than 4 inches, you could use just six roof beams. If your house is larger than 7½ inches in diameter, I recommend using more roof beams. They are a functional yet aesthetic element, and the roof may look weak if there are too few beams in a large house.

### 4 APPLY DECORATIVE TWIGS

Now that the roof beams are in place it is possible to fit a matching pair of decorative twigs to the front and back of the house. Getting the roof beams into position first defines available space for adding decorative twigs without interfering with the roof beams.

### 5 INSTALL TWIG RAFTERS AND EAVES RING

Continue to follow the instructions in Chapter 5 on page 134 and install the roof rafters to create a conical roof for your round house. (You may opt to make a removable roof if you feel confident with your skill level. Just follow those instruction threads instead.)

5

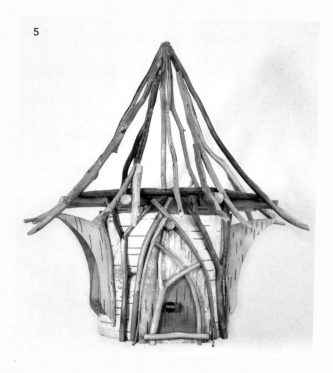

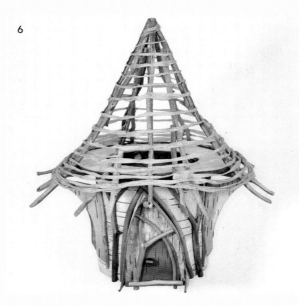

6

## 6 INSTALL UNDERLAYER ROOF SUPPORT

As with the instructions for the framed roof tutorial on page 138, use raffia or a similar material, such as heavy thread, yarn, or cotton string, to apply a webbing surface for your mid-layer of roofing. If the house will be equipped with LED lighting (optional) install the lighting at this stage, either before or after the raffia/paper application as you chose. Follow the basic lighting instructions found in Chapter 4 on page 104 and adapt as you wish for this design.

## 7 COVER THE ROOF WITH THE FELT LAYER

Following the instructions in Chapter 5 on page 138 and apply the felt layer upon which your final decorative roofing layer will be attached. Use brown felt for any bark, pinecone scales, or other dark roofing materials. Use green or appropriate-colored felt for silk botanicals (either leaves and/or flower petals) that will look harmonious with your final roofing materials.

7

8

## 8 APPLY THE FINAL, DECORATED ROOF LAYER

Here we have the finished roof as is described in the tutorial in Chapter 5, page 140, using pinecone scale shingles for the first two layers and silk botanicals for the rest of the roof. Feel free to modify this tutorial and apply whatever roof covering inspires you.

## 9 FINISH THE INTERIOR OF THE HOUSE (IF DESIRED)

This is the view from the bottom of the house so far. For this simple structure, I've chosen to line the main house with a fresh spring green mulberry paper. Using the tracing of the footprint of the house to arrive at the approximate shape and size, make and apply a circle of paper to the ceiling of the room. Next, add the paper to the walls, following the guidelines in Chapter 4, page 117, on finishing the interior. Once the ceiling and the walls are covered with the paper, apply a small decorative strip of printed floral paper to what will be the very top edge of the wall inside the house. (In this example it was approximately ½ inch wide.) This decorative strip acts to camouflage any mismatches between the wallpaper on the ceiling paper. The final touch is to add decorative frames over the window openings on the *inside* to give the interior of the house a nice finish. Any additional decorations, personalization, or other embellishments that you wish to add to the inside of the house must be done now, because the next step will seal up the house completely.

## 10 MAKE THE BASE

You will make a simple, flat base for this house. Using a sheet of cabinet-grade ³⁄₁₆- or ⅛-inch-thick plywood, cut out a pear-shaped base. The size of this base is determined by the footprint of the house, including the bump-out created by the door vestibule. The wood extends out beyond the edge of the house by a small margin, as desired. Place the house on the base, and check to make sure that the house is plumb and level. Trim the bottom edge of the house as needed to make it sit square and level.

Smooth and sand the plywood base to a medium-high finish and then seal with several thin coats of spray urethane. Wait until completely dry to attach to house.

## 11   ATTACH THE BASE AND DECORATIVE TRIMS

Once the house and base have been fully prepared, check the interior one last time. Apply a bead of wood-colored epoxy to the bottom edge of the house, and quickly attach the house to the plywood base. Clean up any excessive glue before dries.

Once the house is permanently attached to the plywood base, you may wish to add a decorative strip of birch bark (or similar material) around the very bottom of the house. This strip will add an extra layer of contact for added strength, and it will also camouflage any gaps in the joint between the house and the base. You will need to apply this strip in pieces as you work around the twigs. As a final touch, cut and glue a small piece of preserved mass in place as a natural welcome mat.

Now is the time to add glass beads and decorative ornaments the roof and exterior walls of your house.

11

12

## 12   MAKE AND ADD A ROOF FINIAL

Follow the instructions in Chapter 5 page 143 which describes how to make and install a finial for this conical roof.

To add bead dangles, use jeweler's head pins or beading wire to create beaded dangles as desired. Glue them into place using epoxy glue.

Your house is now finished and ready to be enjoyed. Congratulations!

# GOLDEN COTTAGE

This tutorial is geared toward the accomplished builder. It is mainly a photo tutorial with minimal instructions, because in order to make it, you need to be familiar with and have practiced many of the building techniques used in this construction. As with all the other tutorials in this book, you can adapt the materials and the process for other creations. Work carefully, and with patience, you can construct this gorgeous house, or one quite like it, with your own touches!

Many of the key elements to make the main house body are made with golden birch bark, but feel free to use any material you like. It just needs to be fairly stiff and rigid. Contrasting twigs for trim will add strength and interest.

1

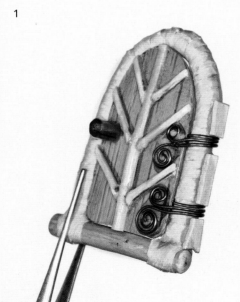

## 1 BUILD THE DOOR

Follow the tutorial in Chapter 3 on page 64 and complete a door scaled to your project.

2

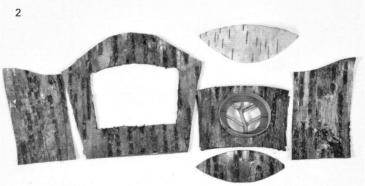

## 2 BUILD THE BAY WINDOW

Build a bay window in the central back panel as described in Chapter 3 on page 90.

### 3 | BUILD SIDE WINDOWS AND INSTALL

Build and install the side windows as described in Chapter 3 on page 83. You can use different mullions if you wish.

3

### 4 | INSTALL LIGHT-BLOCKING FELT AROUND WINDOWS

Apply felt to cover over all construction joints around all the windows. Check all wall panels for any holes and fill.

4

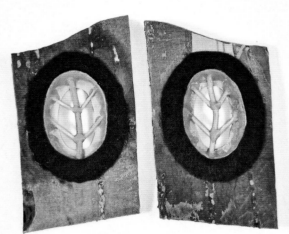

### 5 | INSTALL DOOR AND ADD LIGHT-BLOCKING FABRIC

Make a contrasting frame for the door, using the door as a template. Cut an opening in the front house panel and install the door, just as you did the windows. Apply the frame. Apply light-blocking felt around the door on the inside. Using the panels as templates, cut out wallpaper panels. Cut holes for windows and door while all of the pieces are flat.

5

6

## 6  JOIN SIDE, FRONT, AND BACK PANELS TOGETHER

Use strips of felt to attach the panels together. Fit panels as closely together as possible but leave a little gap for the twig trim to sit in (applied next). The felt provides a flexible joint that is also strong and light-fast. Connect three front panels together and three back panels together.

## 7  APPLY WALLPAPER AND INTERIOR TRIM FRAMES

Apply wallpaper to all the walls (see page 118). Overlap and trim as needed. Apply decorative interior frames around windows and door.

7

## 8  JOIN FRONT TO BACK

Join front to back sections with strips of felt as before (you may need narrower strips than used before as the angle is more acute).

8

## 9 FINISH THE WALLPAPERING

Complete installing wallpaper. The house should still be a little bit flexible.

9

## 10 FINISH TOP EDGE AND ADD TWIG TRIM

Apply trim twigs to all vertical wall joints. Paint the top end before installing to match bark color, if needed. Use a generous bead of epoxy behind each twig. Do one at a time, and attend to drips before they set. Optional trick: If your twig has a fragile bark that you wish to protect, you can apply a thin coat of glue (clear epoxy for a shiny finish, white glue for a matte finish). Apply the sealed twigs to the house walls as described.

10

Front of house.

10

Back of house.

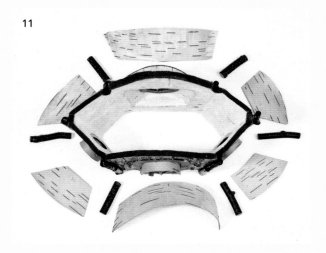

11

## 11 BUILD THE BEAMS AND EAVES RING AND APPLY (TEMPORARILY)

With tiny drops of hot glue, temporarily attach the beams as they rest in the wall section joints with approximately ½ inch of the beam sitting inside the house. Tip: a single drop to the felt edge strip on either side of the twig should be enough. Cut eaves material as shown. (Make a paper template first to get the shapes right.) You can use bark or any stiff, flexible material. The good side is facing down here.

## 12 INSTALL THE BEAMS AND EAVES RING AND STRENGTHEN THE JOINTS

Carefully attach each eaves piece to the beams. Keep all of the glue on the upper side of the ring with none showing below. Do one section at a time, and test to make sure it is not getting stuck to the house. The ring will be very floppy at this point. Attach strips of reinforcing paper to each section, overlapping the beams as shown. Do the entire ring.

With surgical precision, use a sharp knife and cut the ring free from the house. Ideally cut just the drops, not the twigs or the felt.

12

Top view.

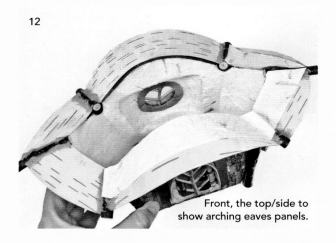

12

Front, the top/side to show arching eaves panels.

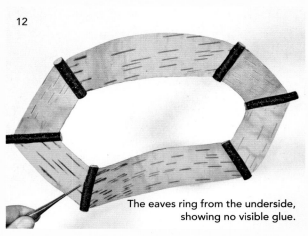

12

The eaves ring from the underside, showing no visible glue.

## 13    CREATE AND INSTALL ROOF LIP AND LIGHT-SEAL THE BEAM JOINTS

13

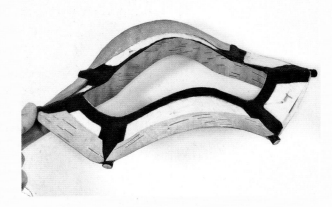

This is a very fiddly step, so go slowly and take your time. Glue the felt strips to the backs of the bark with epoxy and form the strip into a curve similar to the inside of the eaves ring. Do both strips.

Now glue each strip into place as shown. The bark faces in, but the strip will attach firmly to the ends of the beams and the edge of the eaves ring. Glue firmly. Apply strips of felt to all of the joints as shown to block and light and add strength. The roof at this point should slip neatly onto the house edge with the lip sitting inside the house. Trim and adjust.

14

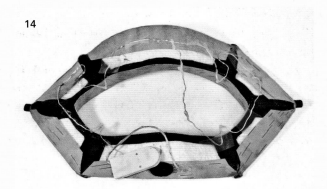

## 14    BEGIN TO INSTALL LIGHTING IN ROOF

Following the instructions in Chapter 4, page 106. Begin to install the lighting. Note that several bulbs are planned for the eaves, four at the inner quadrants (to illuminate the interior) and two bulbs are free to go up inside the cupola. Tack temporarily in place with tape or drops of hot glue.

## 15    CREATE CUPOLA AND WINDOW

Create a round cupola with a window installed. Here it was easier to just line the whole thing with felt for strength and light-blocking. Install window and seal.

15

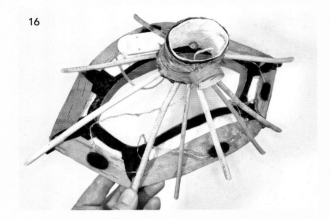

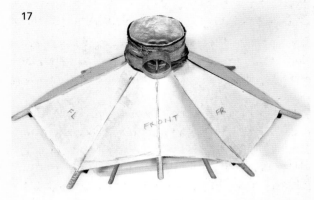

## 16 CREATE FRAME FOR ROOF AND APPLY CUPOLA

Place eaves ring on house. Use a temporary support to float the cupola approximately where you want it above the roof. Use matching quality twigs to create rafters and join cupola to eaves ring, as shown. Glue lightly until all the rafters are in place, then use more glue to secure. Finish installing the lighting wires. Mask the eaves bulbs with felt ovals. Line the cupola with wallpaper and attach the last lights.

## 17 MAKE PATTERN FOR PANELED ROOF AND OPTIONAL DECORATIVE LINER

Make a paper template of entire roof as shown. Label each section carefully.

Cut out nice pieces of bark to match each section. You could also skip the bark and use felt panels if you plan on using silk botanicals, conifer scales, or needle felting for a roof finish. Cut matching pieces of decorative paper (good side facing in) if you want to line the roof. (This is suggested with a bark roof.)

## 18 CREATE BATTERY BOX, APPLY DECORATIVE LINER, AND OUTER ROOF BARK

Make and install a box for the battery unit as shown (see another photo on page 107) in Chapter 3 under Lighting. Attach the cover and seal up (not shown).

Optional: Apply the lining papers to the rafters as shown (green paper). Do all of the roof sections, trimming as needed. Put good side down. Glue securely to rafters all along the length. Seal to eaves ring at wide end.

Apply the bark roof sections as shown on top of the paper liners. Glue firmly. Also attach to the eaves ring if you can do so without distorting the ring.

Glue a ring of felt to the top of the cupola edge.

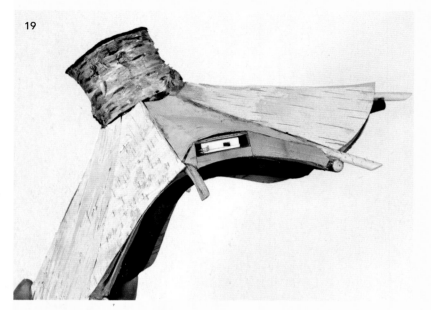

19

## CREATE AND INSTALL EAVES FACADE TRIM

Depending on your materials, the battery box will most likely need a special facade to cover over the entire end of the roof section, between the beams, as shown. This will be visible, so take your time and make it perfect.

Apply your last roof section when finished.

Seal the connection between the bark and the eaves around the entire roof. You can fill with felt or bark strips as desired, but the wide ends of each section between the rafters should be sealed up.

20

## APPLY DECORATIVE TRIMS TO ROOF AND CUPOLA

Apply decorative trim as shown. (The contrasting bark edge and dark twigs in the joints as well as curly bits under the cupola are all optional.) ***Note:*** *Learn from my mistake and do not attach the curls at the ends of the rafters just yet!*

## HOW TO CREATE CUPOLA ROOF

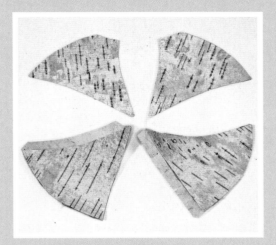

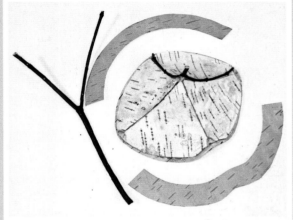

TOP LEFT: Four-piece roof made with bark and paper lining already attached. Create a paper pattern first to get the shape right.

TOP RIGHT: Apply matching trim as with the main roof. Note slight cut-out in the front to go over the round window. This is a small, optional detail.

LEFT: Attach acorn finial using epoxy glue for a secure adhesion. If the small twig trim is not working, you can try thin strips of dark birch bark as shown. Apply curly trim, if desired. Set aside.

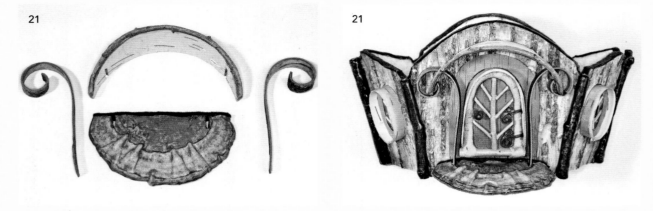

21

## 21 CREATE AND INSTALL STOOP AND PORCH (OPTIONAL)

Cut a piece of curved birch bark as shown, and apply a twig edge. Cut and fit a shelf mushroom to fit under the doorsill. Create a means to connect the two. (I used thick, curled birch bark, but any strong, vertical component will work. Be creative!)

Attach fungus to the house wall under the door. Attach curved porch roof so that your vertical posts will fit in between. Attach vertical posts and bark curls now.

## 22 ATTACH CUPOLA ROOF

Attach the cupola roof with epoxy. Check for light leaks and block with felt strips. Apply faux eaves to the underside of the cupola roof, if desired, before the roof is attached.

## INSTALL INTERIOR DECORATIONS AND fLOOR WITH RUG

TOP LEFT: A piece of white, acid-free foam-core for the floor trimmed to fit perfectly. Green felt for carpet. Brown paper to finish underside (optional). Decorations for the inside!

TOP RIGHT: Install the foam-core floor panel to the bottom of the house, leaving a ½-inch space under the house. From the underside, tack floor panel temporarily in place with small drops of hot glue. Turn the house over to decorate the interior. Apply the decorations, bringing all stem ends to the floor, if possible. When finished, install the carpet and hide the ends of the decorations.

LEFT: Turn house over and finish the bottom. A piece of green felt seals the fungus underside. Attach felt pads to the corners if the house will be standing on any fine furniture without a base.

## 23 MAKE THE BASE

Collect materials for the base: ⅛-inch plywood cut to desired shape, several pieces of felt, preserved moss, and decorations.

23

## 24 APPLY FELT LAYERS FOR CONTOURS

24

You can add layers of felt to make a contoured landscape, or just apply one layer to cover the plywood—your choice. After applying the first flat layer, build layers of green felt around, but not touching, the house.

When sculpted as desired, cover with pieces of preserved moss, cut, and fit as needed. Glue moss down well (hot glue is fine here) to felt.

## 25 DECORATE BASE AND EDGE

Add foliage, stones, flowers, crystals, etc. as desired. Cut a strip of felt and apply to the edge or paint the edge. (Paint before applying any felt layers for best results.)

25

Base, front and back view.

## 26 APPLY CURLY ROOF TRIM (OPTIONAL)

After all construction is completed, now is the best time to add the curly trim at the ends of the rafters.

Now that you've followed these detailed tutorials and step-by-step photo progressions, you should be ready to explore and create your own faerie houses.

Be amazed (and proud)! Enjoy!

Your finished beautiful Golden Cottage, with a door that opens and a roof that removes so visitors can peer inside to enjoy all your creative work. Well done!

# index

## A

Adirondack Faerie Lodge, 16–17
Arched Frame, Hinged Door in an, 64–69
Autumn Leaf Gazebo, 10–11

## B

balconies, 159–160
bark, 48
bark roofs, 128
base layer of roof, 128
bases
    about, 150–151
    as floors, 123–124
    for Golden Cottage, 182–183
    for Green Dreams House, 168–169
    simple, 152–155
battery pack, hiding, 109–110
battery-powered micro LED string lights, 105–108
battery-powered tea lights, 105
bay windows, 76, 90–95, 96, 97
Beach House, 18–19
Bellflower House, 14–15
birch bark samples, 48
branches, 46–47
Brookwater Pavilion, 20–21
building basics, 42–43
building materials, 46–51

## C

Cedar Basket House, 10–11
clear epoxy, 47
collecting materials, 46–49
conversions, 186
coverings for roofs, 128–131
cupola, 176–180
curved walls, 40–41

## D

designing houses, 42
Dogwood Chateau, 18
Dogwood Duplex, 31
doors
    about, 54
    fixed, 54–56, 60–63
    for Golden Cottage, 171
    for Green Dreams House, 165
    hinged, 57–58, 64–69
    Hinged Door in an Arched Frame, 64–69
    "stained glass," 59
    Twig-Framed Fixed Door, 60–63
Dragon Castle, 52–53

## E

eaves, 166, 175
eco-glues, 47
Emerald Moss House, 12–13
epoxy, 47
exterior roof covering, 128

## F

Faerie Château, 36–37
Farmwood Cottage, 14
felt strip, finishing with, 120
finial, 143, 169
finishing touches, 50–51
fixed doors, 54–56, 60–63
flat walls, 40–41
flat-frame style windows, 71
Flat-Framed Window, 80–82
floors, 123–125, 181
flower roofs, live, 129
footbridges, 158–159
Forest Moss Palace, 32–33
fungus roofs, 131
fungus stairs, 157

## G

glue, 47
Golden Cottage, 163, 170–185
Golden Door, 12
Green Dreams House, 162–163, 164–169

## H

High-Summer Cottage Garden House, 17
Hinged Door in an Arched Frame, 64–69
hinged doors, 57–58, 64–69
Hosta Treehouse, 22
hot glue, 38, 47
house styles, 40–41

## I

Ice Queen's Palace, 34–35
indoor faerie houses, 40
interior decorating, 117–119, 168, 173, 181

## L

landscaping, 150–151, 183
latticework, 74
leaf roofs, live, 130
lighting
    about, 101–103
    camouflaging wires for, 110
    embellishments for, 112–116
    for Golden Cottage, 176
    hiding battery pack for, 109–110
    installing, 105–116
    materials for, 104
    windows with, 79
live flower roofs, 129
live leaf roofs, 130
location, 37–40

## M

Marsh House, 23
materials
    building, 46–51
    collecting, 46–49
    lighting, 104
metric equivalents, 186
micro LED string lights, battery-powered, 105–108
middle layer of roof, 128
moss roofs, 130
Mossy Manor House, 24–25
mullion details, 74
mushroom roofs, 131
mushrooms, 49

## N

needle felted roof, 131
No-Frame Removable Roof with Silk Botanicals, 144–149

## O

outdoor faerie houses, 37–39
outdoor toolkit, 44

## P

papers, 51
pathways, 156–157
pinecone scale roofs, 130, 140–141
porches, 96–99, 180
porthole windows, 73, 86–89
projects
    Golden Cottage, 170–185
    Green Dreams House, 164–169
    How to Build a Bay Window, 90–95
    How to Build a Hinged Door in an Arched Frame, 64–69
    How to Build a Twig-Framed Fixed Door with a Simple Surround, 60–63
    How to Create a No-Frame Removable Roof with Silk Botanicals, 144–149
    How to Make a Flat-Framed Window, 80–82
    How to Make a Porthole Window, 86–89
    How to Make a Twig Frame Roof, 132–143
    How to Make a Window with a Frame within a Liner, 83–85

## R

rafters, 136–137, 166
Riverstone Tower, 34
Rivertwig House, 33
roofs
    about, 127–128
    base layer of, 128
    components of, 128
    covering with pine cones and silk botanicals, 140–143
    coverings for, 128–131
    cupola, 176–180
    fungus, 131
    for Golden Cottage, 176–178, 184
    for Green Dreams House, 166–167
    live flower, 129
    live leaf, 130
    middle layer of, 128
    moss, 130
    mushroom, 131
    needle felted, 131
    No-Frame Removable Roof with Silk Botanicals, 144–149
    pinecone scale, 130, 140–141
    removable shelf for, 121
    silk botanical, 129, 142–143, 144–149
    Twig Frame Roof, 132–143

## S

sconces, 112, 116
shelf for roof, removable, 121
silk botanical roofs, 129, 142–143, 144–149
Simple Surround, Twig-Framed Fixed Door
    with a, 60–63
sketches, 42
Spring Gazebo, 30–31
"stained glass" doors, 59
stairs, 156–157
Stone Garden Hut, 28
Stonewood Cottage, 26–27
studio toolkit, 45
Sunflower House, 121–122

## T

tea lights, battery-powered, 105
temperature conversions, 186
tidbits, 49
tiger lily house, 8–9
toolkits, 43–45
top edge, finishing, 120–122, 174
towers, 96–97
Tulip Tea House, 29
Twig Frame Roof, 132–143
twig framed windows, 72
Twig-Framed Fixed Door with a Simple Surround,
    60–63
twiggy bits, 158–160
twigs, 46–47

## W

wall coverings/wallpaper, 51, 117–119, 173–174
window seats, 94
windows
    about, 70–95
    bay, 76, 90–95, 171
    flat-frame style, 71, 80–82
    general instructions for, 70
    for Golden Cottage, 171–172
    for Green Dreams House, 165
    with lighting, 79
    mullion details for, 74–75
    porthole, 73, 86–89
    in stone houses, 77–78
    styles of, 70–73
    twig framed, 72
    Window with a Frame within a Liner, 83–85
wires, camouflaging, 110
wood-colored epoxy, 47

# about the author

**B**orn the eldest of three equally talented daughters to an architect/nature photographer father and a mother with a lifelong passion for flowers and gardens, I was destined to have a deep reverence for the environment and an innate understanding of what the Japanese call *wabi-sabi*: the art of finding beauty in the imperfections and elegance of nature, of accepting the natural cycles of flourishing growth and decay/death.

My early years were spent blissfully engaged with all manners of creativity and adventure as I grew up in the forests, pastures, and gardens of Shelburne Farms in Shelburne, Vermont. In those days we were given complete freedom to play in and explore the hundreds of acres surrounding our rural home and the mythic buildings that dotted the farm—relics of the late nineteenth century Gilded Age designed by the prominent architect Robert H. Robertson. I believe that growing up with these remarkable buildings and out in the wilds of nature laid the seeds for what would later become my art/career path of expression: the building of faerie houses and other environmental sculpture works.

As with all mythic adventures, the traveler must go away before they can return home, and so it was with me. I was fortunate to be able to make my living as a professional watercolor artist for over 22 years and to travel to many sacred and magical locations. I also explored the internal landscape with deep excursions into mythology, meditation, and ancient studies, which captured my imagination and fed back into the matrix of my creative work.

Having returned to the northern forests once more, this book offers an opportunity to share some of the technical skills I have developed along the way. I love living on the fringe of what is considered "normal" and continue to thrive in the liminal spaces between the visible and invisible realms, where magic still exists and the flow of timelessness is experienced regularly. I am a bridge person, of that I am sure . . . The rest is still a work in progress.

**Sally J. Smith**
www.greenspiritarts.com
www.greenspiritarts.blogspot.com

# conversions

## Metric Equivalent

| | 1/64 | 1/32 | 1/25 | 1/16 | 1/8 | 1/4 | 3/8 | 2/5 | 1/2 | 5/8 | 3/4 | 7/8 | 1 | 2 | 3 | 4 | 5 | 6 | 7 | 8 | 9 | 10 | 11 | 12 | 36 | 39.4 |
|---|---|---|---|---|---|---|---|---|---|---|---|---|---|---|---|---|---|---|---|---|---|---|---|---|---|---|
| Inches (in.) | 1/64 | 1/32 | 1/25 | 1/16 | 1/8 | 1/4 | 3/8 | 2/5 | 1/2 | 5/8 | 3/4 | 7/8 | 1 | 2 | 3 | 4 | 5 | 6 | 7 | 8 | 9 | 10 | 11 | 12 | 36 | 39.4 |
| Feet (ft.) | | | | | | | | | | | | | | | | | | | | | | | | 1 | 3 | 3 1/12 |
| Yards (yd.) | | | | | | | | | | | | | | | | | | | | | | | | | 1 | 1 1/12 |
| Millimeters (mm) | 0.40 | 0.79 | 1 | 1.59 | 3.18 | 6.35 | 9.53 | 10 | 12.7 | 15.9 | 19.1 | 22.2 | 25.4 | 50.8 | 76.2 | 101.6 | 127 | 152 | 178 | 203 | 229 | 254 | 279 | 305 | 914 | 1,000 |
| Centimeters (cm) | | | | | | | 0.95 | 1 | 1.27 | 1.59 | 1.91 | 2.22 | 2.54 | 5.08 | 7.62 | 10.16 | 12.7 | 15.2 | 17.8 | 20.3 | 22.9 | 25.4 | 27.9 | 30.5 | 91.4 | 100 |
| Meters (m) | | | | | | | | | | | | | | | | | | | | | | | | .30 | .91 | 1.00 |

## Converting Measurements

| TO CONVERT: | TO: | MULTIPLY BY: |
|---|---|---|
| Inches | Millimeters | 25.4 |
| Inches | Centimeters | 2.54 |
| Feet | Meters | 0.305 |
| Yards | Meters | 0.914 |
| Miles | Kilometers | 1.609 |
| Square inches | Square centimeters | 6.45 |
| Square feet | Square meters | 0.093 |
| Square yards | Square meters | 0.836 |
| Cubic inches | Cubic centimeters | 16.4 |
| Cubic feet | Cubic meters | 0.0283 |
| Cubic yards | Cubic meters | 0.765 |
| Pints (U.S.) | Liters | 0.473 (Imp. 0.568) |
| Quarts (U.S.) | Liters | 0.946 (Imp. 1.136) |
| Gallons (U.S.) | Liters | 3.785 (Imp. 4.546) |
| Ounces | Grams | 28.4 |
| Pounds | Kilograms | 0.454 |
| Tons | Metric tons | 0.907 |

| TO CONVERT: | TO: | MULTIPLY BY: |
|---|---|---|
| Millimeters | Inches | 0.039 |
| Centimeters | Inches | 0.394 |
| Meters | Feet | 3.28 |
| Meters | Yards | 1.09 |
| Kilometers | Miles | 0.621 |
| Square centimeters | Square inches | 0.155 |
| Square meters | Square feet | 10.8 |
| Square meters | Square yards | 1.2 |
| Cubic centimeters | Cubic inches | 0.061 |
| Cubic meters | Cubic feet | 35.3 |
| Cubic meters | Cubic yards | 1.31 |
| Liters | Pints (U.S.) | 2.114 (Imp. 1.76) |
| Liters | Quarts (U.S.) | 1.057 (Imp. 0.88) |
| Liters | Gallons (U.S.) | 0.264 (Imp. 0.22) |
| Grams | Ounces | 0.035 |
| Kilograms | Pounds | 2.2 |
| Metric tons | Tons | 1.1 |

## Converting Temperatures

Convert degrees Fahrenheit (F) to degrees Celsius (C) by following this simple formula: Subtract 32 from the Fahrenheit temperature reading. Then multiply that number by 5/9. For example, 77°F - 32 = 45. 45 × 5/9 = 25°C.

To convert degrees Celsius to degrees Fahrenheit, multiply the Celsius temperature reading by 9/5, then add 32. For example, 25°C × 9/5 = 45. 45 + 32 = 77°F.

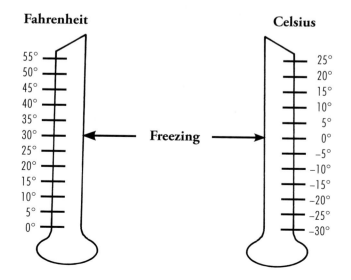